CIVILIZING YOUR PUPPY

Second Edition

Barbara J. Wrede

with 86 Photographs

Illustrations by
Michele Earle-Bridges

BARRON'S

Cover Photos

Front cover: an eight-week-old bloodhound; inside front cover: a seven-week-old beagle; inside back cover: a 14-week-old springer spaniel; back cover: a six-week-old English bulldog

All inquiries should be addressed to:
Barron's Educational Series, Inc.
250 Wireless Boulevard
Hauppauge, New York 11788

International Standard Book No. 0-8120-9787-4

Library of Congress Catalog Card No. 96-32935

Library of Congress Cataloging-in-Publication Data
Wrede, Barbara, 1931–
    Civilizing your puppy / Barbara J. Wrede ; illustrations by Michele Earle-Bridges.—2nd ed.
        p.   cm.
    Includes bibliographical references and index.
    ISBN 0-8120-9787-4
    1. Dogs—Training. I. Title.
 SF431.W74   1997
636.7'0887—dc20   96-32935
                                                          CIP

Printed in Hong Kong
98765

About the Author

Barbara J. Wrede has lived with puppies and dogs all her life. The cocker spaniels of her young years were replaced first by boxers, then by weimaraners, and finally by a multitude of Great Danes. Wrede has held obedience training classes for all breeds of dogs, but more significantly, she has spent hours helping puppy and dog owners solve canine training problems that threatened the optimum bonding between dog and owner. While she was actively breeding and selling dogs, she compiled many pages of training and care suggestions for people all over North America who had obtained puppies from her. Those personal recipes for living happily with puppies were the genesis of this book.

Acknowledgments

While completing this book, I received help and encouragement from several people whom I want to thank. Chief among these is my editor, Don Reis, whose sense of humor and perceptive guidance kept me enthusiastic about the project. Lillian Steinfeld reawakened my zeal for excellence in presentation by her unswerving commitment to perfection. And with her careful reading and strong suggestions, Helgard Niewisch, DVM, helped me to focus this book more sharply. And my husband, Kent, deserves praise for pretending not to notice when the project made me crazy.

Note

This book deals with the acquisition and keeping of dogs. The publisher considers it important to point out that the rules of dog keeping set forth in this book apply primarily to normally developed young dogs from a good breeder; that is, to healthy animals with good character traits. Owing to bad experiences with humans, some dogs may have peculiar behavior or may tend to bite. These dogs should be taken in only by experienced dog owners. Even well-trained and carefully supervised dogs may cause damage to someone else's property or even cause accidents. Sufficient insurance coverage is in your own interest. In any case, taking out a dog liability policy for your pet is strongly recommended.

Contents

Foreword

The family dog is an important member of any household. We spend billions of dollars and thousands of hours annually on our canine family members. Most of the time, we're rewarded with love and companionship that can't be equalled. But to make the most of this special relationship between dog and family, a great deal of early training is necessary. Unfortunately—I might even say "criminally"—in the United States we kill hundreds of thousands of puppies and dogs every year in dog shelters and pounds; in addition, some are abandoned to die slow, agonizing deaths. This tragic waste of life is largely due to people who get puppies and neglect to socialize and train them to grow up to be loving and beloved members of a family. With a little work and the correct knowledge and attitude, puppies can be turned into wonderful, cooperative pets in only a few months. This book is a distillation of advice, tips, strategies, and actual classes I have provided over a period of more than 20 years. Nothing here is theoretical. All has been tested in the homes of countless new puppies or older dogs that have been rescued.

Child and adult, I have been in a family that raised dogs for more than half a century. When I was small, my family raised cocker spaniels, the last of whom died when I was a junior in college. Cockers were followed by boxers, a breed that are the most humor-loving dogs I know. As an adult I spent several years in the company of weimaraners, those ghostly gray German hunting dogs that are the most intelligent dogs I've ever experienced. However, as time went by, I found that the weimaraners I owned demanded a stronger disciplinary hand than I prefer to use on dogs, and I phased out of weimaraners and into Great Danes. The Danes have been the constant companions of my husband Kent and me for over 20 years. Although all puppies need early training, because they grow so big so fast, Dane puppies can be more obviously out of hand without training than, say, cocker puppies. When an untrained lout of a 50-pound pup jumps on your frail old great-auntie, the impact is more serious!

Thus, through need, I've become an expert on getting a big, klutzy puppy off to a good start. Having been more or less responsible for well over 100 Great Danes, plus a dozen or so weimaraners and at least as many boxers, I know most of the scams we humans can use to foil intelligent, energetic, and enthusiastic puppies—and without breaking their spirits or making them into windup toys. Besides being an obedience class trainer, I've dealt with thousands of telephone calls. Most of those calls start with some version of, "I just got this puppy, and you won't believe what it's just done! Can you help?" I've also worked as a volunteer in an animal shelter and seen firsthand the sad and unnecessary abandonment of basically fine dogs and puppies.

Special attention is given to the needs of the giant breeds—Danes, Newfoundlands, St. Bernards, Great Pyrenees, giant schnauzers— because these dogs have special dietary and training needs while they're pups. There is also some emphasis on the more hardheaded, stubborn dogs like weimaraners and other sporting breeds, because those dogs are brighter and more energetic than the more placid breeds and hence present a greater challenge to the new owner. Be aware, though, that whatever applies to the big or energetic breeds also applies, scaled-down, to all breeds including mixed breeds. My phone calls and training classes have included all breeds of dogs, including those of mixed parentage. This is a sort of dog training cookbook—use those recipes that fit your chosen dog and your preferred way of living.

In the book you'll meet some first-rate dogs. Tops in the brilliant and stubborn category is Bucky, my last weimaraner, whom I dearly loved and who at times taught me more than I wanted to know about what mischief a dog can devise. There's also Bucky's mother, Heidi, who taught me to overcome the Hopeless Digger Syndrome. Of the Danes you'll meet, there's Killer, that goofy blue marshmallow of a male Dane who fell into trouble and wondered how he got there. And there's Captain Ahab (Cappy), the first Dane puppy that I had from its birth.

Mostly what you'll meet in this book are the answers to your puppy-training questions. Ideally you'll learn those answers before problems become serious. As you use this book, more and more you'll find yourself able to think like a dog, which gives you a nice edge when it comes to heading off problems before they start.

My lifelong thanks go to people like "Deck" Deckrosh, Tony and Eileen Perreault, and others who shared with me their dog lore so that I can share it with you. Most especially I want to thank Dr. George Browne, formerly of Ferndale, California, who, until his death in May, 1987, was the veterinarian who took care of my Great Danes and taught me in a way that goes far beyond simple textbook knowledge. Much of what I pass on here comes from George Browne, who cared passionately for animals.

Barbara J. Wrede
Fortuna, California

Preface to the Second Edition

It's true that you can, indeed, teach old dogs new tricks. It's equally true that long-time dog trainers can learn new things, and that's why I've seen the need for a second edition of *Civilizing Your Puppy*.

The first thing I realized is that I had to emphasize how important it is for the owner/trainer to learn to rap out a good, strong NO. Of all the shortcomings in training that I see, it's the inability to say a credible NO that dooms too many people to ineffectiveness as trainers. Practice, practice, until you can say NO in a way that your dog can NOT fail to understand.

Right on the heels of this comes the matter of dominance. The week after the first edition of this book came out, I acquired the most dominant Great Dane I've every had. Cordy was seven months old, 130 pounds (59 kg), and 28 inches (71 cm) at the shoulder when I brought him home, and he believed that the world was, as the cliche has it, his oyster. I had to establish dominance more firmly than I've had to, and I quickly succeeded. Kent, my husband, did not work on the dominance factor, and to this day, he does not get quick response when he tells Cordy to do something.

The growth of the Internet brought me into contact with people who have questions about their dogs' training and behavior. Very soon I recognized that many new puppy owners equate training with cruelty—and hence do not train their puppies until the pups are woefully out of hand. Besides posting responses on the 'Net, I decided that is was time to update this book, emphasizing that training can and should be done with love, consistency, and firmness. There is neither the need nor the excuse for cruelty. And high in the cruelty department I place *not* training—for the untrained puppy grows into the unbearable dog who is either banished to the end of a chain in the backyard or taken to a dog pound and killed. I don't consider either of those fates kind or loving.

There are also product updates since the first edition, especially in the realm of external parasite control. We humans might actually be winning the war on fleas!

Finally, I had to eat a little crow. Before, I said that I saw no reason ever for pinch (or prong) collars. I take that back—with reservations. But there are times when only the prong collar is going to get the job done, and you'll learn about them in this edition.

The book is still about teaching puppies to be fit members of your human pack. However, I realize that we're all engaged in a lifetime of learning—puppies, dogs, and the people who love and value them. With the marvels of instant electronic communication, you can leave messages for me. My cyberspace address is Giorge@aol.com. I'll get back to you, often the same day.

As we'd say if we were doing the Iditarod together, Mush on!

Fortuna, California
July, 1996

Chapter One
Off to a Good Start

You're the Leader

Taking over the care of a puppy that will grow up into a bona fide adult dog involves a lot more than just buying a sack of dog food and a few puppy toys. Bear in mind that you are now your puppy's leader, teacher, and ultimate guide. In a dog family, there is always a pack leader, sometimes referred to as the *alpha dog.* Puppies look to the leader for direction in every aspect of their behavior. Their leader teaches them essentially how to be a dog—how to be an acceptable member of the pack or family. You are now that leader, and your puppy expects you to teach it how to be an acceptable member of your family. If you do not accept this responsibility, first, your puppy will lose faith in you. Second, and with even more dire consequences, your pup will figure out on its own what's okay and what isn't. Your pup will grow into an ill-taught alpha dog, following its own desires first and foremost. Left to its own devices long enough, it will come to resent not only whatever training you may eventually decide to give it, but even human interference of any

A puppy's mother teaches it how to behave.

kind. Beyond a certain point, such a dog cannot be brought back to dependable socialization. It is often a lack of early training that dooms dogs later to dog pounds, as most people are not up to insisting on alpha status with a stubborn dog that isn't going to give up its authority without a fight.

What, specifically, does it mean for you to insist on being the leader, or the alpha dog? In a nutshell, you decide what behavior you'll encourage in your pup and what behavior you will not tolerate. Let me suggest that you begin with two common puppy behaviors: 1) Biting or chewing on people, and 2) jumping on people. The reason I start with these is that both are alpha behaviors. Both let the pup be dominant to you. If allowed, they give your pup the idea that it is your superior—that it owns you, as it were. When the puppy thinks that, your training is going to be a lot more difficult than if the puppy has already accepted you as top dog.

Let me give you an example. I bought Cordy, a blue Great Dane, when he was seven months old. At that point, he stood about 28 inches (71 cm) at his shoulder and weighed 130 pounds (59 kg). He was a lot of dog. He was—and is—also a remarkably bright dog, able to figure out, for instance, how to push up the latch on a chainlink gate and open the gate. He's also high-spirited, a trait I love and would not change. This combination, however, makes training a real challenge. Add to that the fact that Cordy already had

habits I don't like. For example, I don't like dogs to paw at me, something Cordy did. Further, he resented my correction of that behavior and growled at me, which is totally unacceptable.

I thought about his pawing and his dominant reaction to my corrections. Training a puppy isn't like repairing a car. There isn't one manual that deals with everything for every dog for every instance, as there is with repairing, say, your Buick Grand National's transmission. Each of us has to look at the given behavior and think through what is going on in the canine mind. Then we can correct the behavior and change the thought process. So I pondered Cordy's pawing, and I found my answer. He pawed me *only* when he was sitting next to me on the couch. In that position, his head was higher than mine. He dominated me in a literal one-up position, and in his puppy mind, he also dominated me as alpha. As soon as I stood up, I was taller than he and assumed the one-up position. He never pawed me when I was higher than he, nor did he growl at me then, either.

Having figured out what was going on, I made sure that Cordy didn't have the chance to be taller than me for several months, during which time I impressed on his young mind who was who. He was the subordinate, I was the leader. I didn't allow him to sit next to me on the couch until he had it clear that I was the leader. I gave him no opportunity to be the top dog physically. Now that he's an adult and clear on what I want, he can sit on the couch or snuggle in bed without displaying dominant behavior.

I was fortunate to have civilized countless other puppies before I was faced with Cordy, for if I'd allowed his dominant behavior to continue, I'd very soon have had a dog I could not have controlled.

Thus, if you guide and correct your puppy right from the start, you'll end up with a dream dog that understands and even seems to anticipate your every command. Forming good habits early is easier and more gentle than breaking bad habits in an older puppy or dog. However, it is not true that you can't teach new things to an older dog. It just takes more time, sharper reinforcements, and more of your energy. It is the rare dog that can't learn.

Training a puppy aims at three major goals:

1. Teaching your puppy what you can live with comfortably.
2. Bringing out the best traits of whatever breed your puppy is a member.
3. Socializing your puppy to live within a human "pack."

Straight Home

Home is the first place for you after you've picked up your puppy from the breeder. It's tempting to show off a new puppy, stopping at this relative's

Get your puppy directly to its new home.

house and that friend's shop. However, your puppy is in a state of mild shock. It has just been separated from its entire family, including the only other humans it has known. What it needs most right now is to find out where it lives and who are its new family. Especially if you have a young pup, around eight weeks, its attention span is pretty short. Drag it around to three or four different places and it won't know which end is up. The thing you want most is a family dog who knows where home is and who hangs out there. Thus, you begin on the right foot—you go home!

There's a health reason, too, for not fiddlefooting all over the place. Your pup's resistance to diseases is at a low ebb. Whatever protection it had from its mother's immunizations is beginning to wear off. You don't want to risk exposing it to infectious

Cats and dogs can learn to be good friends.

diseases prior to proper immunization, which will take several weeks. The stress of being separated from mother and littermates makes it additionally vulnerable. A quiet time at home getting settled in and finding out what caring people it's living with is the right prescription now.

Animal Introductions

Even more care needs to be taken with introducing a new puppy to your current pets than in introducing the pup to the human members of your family. A bad first experience with other family pets can set up problems for you down the line.

Older dogs differ, of course, in how readily they accept a new puppy into the home. All will adjust if you're careful and considerate in how you present the puppy. Many an older dog has found a new lease on life with the advent of a frisky,

curious puppy. Our elderly Dane, Tucker, had been more or less creaking around when we got the four-month-old Dane Pinocchio. Within a week of Pinocchio's arrival, Tucker had perked up and was happily showing the new kid where the best parts of the yard were and where to take the most comfortable naps. Tucker even worked up to an occasional playful tug-of-war when Pinocchio offered a pulltoy. Both the older dog and the puppy should be restrained at their first meeting. Have the adult dog on leash in case it snaps at the puppy. Hold the puppy on your lap so it's not in an uncomfortably one-down position vis-a-vis the big dog. Pet both dogs, and use a calming voice. Don't let the puppy jump all over the older dog or paw at it. After a brief introduction, put the older dog in its crate or wherever it generally sleeps; and put the puppy, who may be tired, in the box you're going to have it sleep in. Don't fuss over the puppy to the exclusion of the older dog, as you'll be setting up a jealousy situation.

Make sure that all interactions between dog and puppy are supervised in the first few days. Aggressiveness on the dog's part must be discouraged, but neither can the pup be allowed to romp all over the dog. The two will decide who's down and who's up all in good time. Your job now is to make sure the older dog doesn't feel dethroned and that the puppy isn't browbeaten. Be evenhanded with attention and treats. Don't leave the two alone together

until you're sure that the older dog has accepted the puppy.

Do not allow the puppy to eat out of the dog's dish or to nose around the adult while it's eating. This is almost certain to cause understandable aggressiveness on the older dog's part and sets up a negative situation around feeding times. Neither should the adult be able to steal from the puppy. With two dogs, you're going to have to supervise feeding times at least until both dog and puppy know that they do not trade dishes or hassle each other during meals.

Incidentally, while two kittens are a lot easier to cope with than one kitten, the same is categorically not true of puppies. Two puppies are four times as much trouble as one! What they learn from each other are new ways to drive you crazy. Trust me on this!

On the other hand, the older dog, used to your routine and knowledgeable about your tolerances, will teach the pup a lot. People who use dogs to herd stock often work a puppy with a seasoned older dog. Be aware, though, that any bad habits that you've let your older dog develop will be aped by the puppy. Your abilities as alpha are going to be tested.

Dogs and cats are not natural enemies. Puppies, however, are endlessly curious and often rash. Make sure you introduce the puppy carefully to your resident cat, restraining the pup from pouncing on the cat, and making sure the cat has a ready escape route should the pup get too rambunctious. Again, keep the initial meeting brief. Don't force things.

Don't let the puppy eat the cat's food, either.

We had the ideal puppy-training cat in our big black neutered male, Spunky. Spunky would sit sleepy-eyed as Dane pups swarmed up to him. If any nosed him too rudely, Spunky would put one front paw on the pup's nose and push a little. The second time a pup was rude, Spunky would again put up the paw, but this time, he'd flex the claws out a little, allowing the pup a glimpse of his arsenal. If there was a third time, Spunky reared back and swatted the offending puppy on the nose, claws fully extended. There never was a fourth time.

Puppies and kittens together are the best comedy act there is. The pup is blatantly, endlessly curious. The kitten is equally curious, but guileful. Watching the byplay between a kitten and a puppy is better than most comedy shows I've seen on TV. Many cats come to love their dogs; in fact, we've had cats that liked their dogs better than they did us.

A really assorted mix of pets can live peacefully and happily together. But you, the owner of the menagerie, absolutely must put in some serious supervising and training time at the beginning to make this become a

In a group, puppies comfort each other.

reality. Always remember—not letting bad habits get started is vastly easier than breaking them after they've become ingrained.

Lonesome Pup

When I was studying other people's rules for bringing up well-adjusted dogs, I read a lot of advice about setting up some sort of isolation ward for the new puppy where it couldn't do any harm to the house. "Teach the dog where it belongs right from the start" was the advice of those alleged experts. Well, my idea of living with dogs is that we share a house, except when we're training a litter of several puppies. I spend as little time as possible in the laundry room, as I suspect you do, too. Yet the most commonly suggested spot to isolate the newly arrived puppy is the laundry room! Why would we make a puppy stay there? I suggest making a box or bed for a new puppy, with some old blankets or towels in it for bedding. In Chapter 3, I'll teach you about the crate, which is a species of box. Keep the box pretty much where the people in the family are. You're accomplishing two parts of a training program without your pup being really aware that it's learning anything. First, you're teaching that being near its people is the place of choice, and second, you're getting the pup used to you and your family. You also can begin teaching words. Every time you put Puppy in its box,

say "In your BOX," and pet Puppy as it settles down in the box. Before long, you'll be able to send Puppy to his or her box simply by saying, "BOX."

Especially at night, a new pup is going to be very lonely. It has been used to cuddling up warmly with several other puppy bodies, feeling their twitches and hearing their breathing through the night. Off somewhere in a strange, silent room, Puppy will be scared, unhappy, and sure the world has turned sour. I start new puppies off at night sleeping on my bed. Not only is the puppy more secure and happy, but if it does need to void during the night, I wake up and take it to the right place for that activity. There's something amazingly more friendly and comforting in having a new puppy twitching and snoring on my bed than having a miserable, scared pup howling out its fear and frustration in a locked ward somewhere.

Although this method has worked for me, having a puppy sleep with you may not be your style. No problem. Putting that handy box beside your bed accomplishes the same aims. There's still the early bonding going on, you're not worrying about what the puppy is doing, and everyone gets a good night's sleep.

Every puppy I've ever known has chosen its own sleeping place in its own good time, so I don't spend my life with big floppy Danes taking up more than their share of the bed. Very soon, a pup decides it wants to

sleep in its own place, and your bed becomes perhaps a place it hops onto at your invitation, but not its habitual nighttime sleeping spot.

You both begin your years together on a happier note if you forget all the bad advice about isolating your new pup. You can take some dog hairs on the bed and maybe sop

Puppies cuddle when they sleep with their littermates.

Don't isolate your new puppy. Keep it near you so it won't be lonesome.

up a few puppy puddles, or you wouldn't have acquired a puppy in the firstplace, right? And if you're still mourning the death of a beloved old dog, that new puppy on the bed makes the night less dark. So go ahead—you're not "spoiling" your pup. You're starting right.

What's for Lunch? Feeding Pointers

Here are some tips on starting your puppy right so it becomes an eager eater and doesn't beg from the table.

My Dish, My Place

Begin right away always feeding Puppy from the same dish. You may already have dishes from a former dog. As long as these have been thoroughly cleansed, they'll be fine. Stainless steel bowls are my choice for two reasons. They can't be chewed easily, and they can be thoroughly cleaned. Plastic is under some suspicion because it may harbor disease organisms. If you have to buy new, buy stainless steel.

As well as teaching Puppy from Day One that s/he always eats from the same dish, always feed your pup in the same place. Since Puppy is likely to be distractable at first, somewhere out of the immediate traffic pattern is advisable. Again, you can teach words now, even though at first your puppy may not seem to comprehend. As you set the dish down, announce, "Come get your dinner!" Your pup will soon associate the words with food. Be sure to get your puppy's attention as you put the feeding dish down, for you want a dog that slicks up its meals within a few minutes. Food that stands around is likely to spoil. Furthermore, when you know what Puppy is eating, you can monitor its general health.

Be On Time

Puppies thrive on consistency. Part of teaching a pup to be an eager eater is to maintain a schedule. If you feed the pup at, say, 7:00 A.M. and 5:30 P.M., maintain that schedule whether it's a work day, Sunday, or a vacation at Aunt Sophie's. Not that you have to be slavish to the tenth of a second, of course, but keep to within a half hour of the schedule you're setting. Your puppy will come to expect meals at those set times, be hungry at those times, and, eventually, has-

Keep food and water bowls out of the heavy traffic pattern.

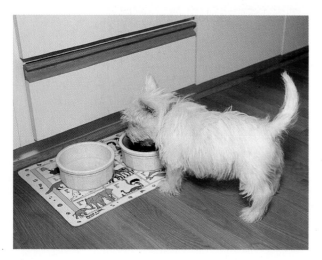

sle you if you don't get the food served at the expected times!

Ten minutes is enough time for a hungry puppy to slurp up its food without having to rush. If the puppy walks away from food left in its dish, you might try coaxing it back to finish, especially if this is early in your life together and you don't yet know exactly how much Puppy eats. Do not, however, add tidbits to the abandoned food in order to coax the puppy back to the bowl. Doing that teaches that you can be conned into behavior that may not be in the dog's best interests. It's a certain way to create a finicky eater.

Once you're sure the puppy is finished eating or, if you've left the food dish down for ten minutes or so and the puppy has walked away, pick up the dish and whatever food may be left over and do not feed the puppy again until the next meal. Throw away the leftover food to avoid contamination, wash the bowl well, and reduce the amount you prepare for the next meal. Ideally, a puppy eats what it will eagerly clean up in ten minutes at each meal. If your pup seems hungry after each meal, or is looking thin and ribby, increase the amount you're feeding. Every puppy has its own metabolism; even littermates will eat different amounts.

Not at the Table

Though Puppy may grow up secure in the knowledge that all table scraps will end up in her/his dish, as far as feeding from the table

goes, DON'T START! Nothing to eat EVER comes directly from the table to Puppy. Cappy, who was a true 38 inches (1 m)-at-the shoulder black Dane, could walk over to the dining room table and look down comfortably into anyone's plate. He did this, however, only to first-time dinner guests, always hoping, I suppose, that they didn't know the rule about dogs not eating at the table. I always told the guest to tell Cappy, "NO!" Some, intimidated by his size and intense scrutiny, managed only a squeaky little "no," which Cappy ignored. When they'd worked up to a fine, serious "NO," Cappy would sigh, turn away, and fling himself on the floor, knowing that once again his ploy had failed. He never begged again from that person. He did learn, though, that visiting children were

Begging at the table quickly becomes an obnoxious habit.

apt to drop a tasty crumb or two, so he always took up a waiting position under the table close enough to a child's chair to sneak out a big tongue and slurp up whatever came his way. If your puppy begs at the table, poking its nose in your lap or pawing you, push it away and say a big "NO!" Should the begging continue and the puppy not yet know the "Go!" command, you can put it in its box. Insist that it stay there as long as you're eating. At the end of the meal, tell the puppy to "Come!" and give it whatever treat you've saved—in another room! Thus you are breaking the begging habit; teaching Puppy that mealtime is a time to leave you alone; and rewarding good behavior.

Snacks?

There are dozens of dog snacks on the market. I'm not so concerned here about their nutritional value as I am about their nuisance value in your program of teaching your puppy to be an eager eater. You can't be sure that your pup is getting the right amount and quality in its basic diet if it is also snacking between meals. So, until you become sure how much your new puppy eats normally to have proper nutrition for its rapidly growing young body, hold the snacks. Many people give snacks to their puppies as reward for good behavior. Indeed, good behavior, such as coming when called, should always be rewarded. Be assured that your joyous approval, expressed with a pat, a hug, and a

cheerful, "Good dog!" are light years more important to your puppy than any snack could be.

Like so many other aspects of puppy training, snacks are something you may want to work up to—after you've carefully set the good habits you want for your pup's lifetime. Many show dogs are trained to exhibit alertness by means of liver snacks held at just the correct distance to get the dog's interest. That's a very specialized use of snacks. I had an old cocker spaniel who wanted a dog biscuit before she'd go to bed at night, a habit she had developed because some of the family always snacked before going to bed. It was a harmless and rather endearing crotchet in an old dog who was already a fine, eager eater of her regular meals. So I'm not condemning all snacking, but I am suggesting that you hold the snacks until you've set the good basic pattern of eating.

How Often?

I've spoken about meals, plural. By the time puppies can leave their littermates, they're on three meals a day—morning, noon, and evening. As soon as a puppy starts dawdling, I suggest that it's time to eliminate lunch. However, I suggest that you maintain a schedule of two meals a day throughout your puppy's life. For the larger breeds, dividing the daily food requirements into two portions reduces the chance of overloading the dog's stomach and thus encouraging gastric torsion. For any breed of dog, being fed is a sign of human care, a high point in the day, and the negligible trouble of feeding a dog twice a day is more than made up by your better ability to oversee your dog's well-being. Especially for a dog that has to be at home alone during the work week, two feedings a day help offset the loneliness.

Water

Free access to plenty of clean water is important to your pup. Some experts suggest restricting water in the evening, supposedly to minimize Puppy's need to eliminate during the night. Our experience has been that as soon as a pup is physically able to control its bladder for several hours, it sleeps through the night. Until that time, we treat a puppy the same way

many parents treat their young children; we wake the puppy up and take it outside to relieve itself just before we go to bed.

Start out right as far as where Puppy gets water. As with having its own food dish, a puppy also needs its own water bowl. Make sure it's a *big* water bowl, as dogs drink a lot of water. A housekeeping tip I'll share with you is to set the water bowl in a larger, more shallow container. I use a dishpan. This keeps the water from being slopped all over the floor; many dogs are sloppy drinkers all their lives.

A puppy will learn quickly where its water bowl is. As with always feeding in the same place, always keep the water bowl filled with clean water in the same place. Puppy learns quickly that this is where s/he gets a drink.

The toilet is not an acceptable source of drinking water for your puppy. No matter how scrupulously you clean your toilet, there are unwelcome intestinal bacteria in toilet water. And if you use one of the continuous cleaner chemicals in

Give your pup plenty of clean water, but don't put the dish where you'll trip over it.

Proper house-breaking is worth every minute you invest in it.

and grief in a family with a new puppy. More dogs end up at pounds because of not being properly housebroken than for any other single reason. This is one aspect of training a new puppy that deserves your fullest commitment, because with three or four days of serious work, you'll reap benefits that will amply reward you throughout your pup's life.

Keep this firmly in mind: When an eight-week-old (or so) puppy eats, drinks, wakes up, or finishes playing, it has to empty its bladder. Basically, what you do first is train yourself! When any one of these events occurs, pick Puppy up, tell it firmly that it's time to Go Potty—or whatever term you're going to use—and take it to the correct place. Supervise until Puppy goes, then praise: "GOOD Puppy!" Make a big deal of praising.

I generally begin a young pup with paper training. Put a thick padding of newspapers on linoleum near the door that's going to be the OUT door later. Then put Puppy on the papers, and go through the rest of the drill: "Go POTTY," emphasizing the operative command, POTTY. When the pup squats elsewhere, grab it up with loud NOs, cart it to the papers, and tell it firmly, "Go POTTY!" I've found that with my dogs, three days of this drill results in a puppy that scrambles off toward the newspapers as soon as it feels the urge to piddle. Sometimes the pup gets only one foot or so actually on the newspaper, but you can see

your toilet tank, think about what years of drinking water with diluted chemical toilet cleaners will do to a dog!

If you get an older puppy that has been accustomed to drinking out of the toilet, the simplest remedy is to close the lid when the toilet isn't in use. Introducing the older pup to where you keep its water bowl and making the toilet unavailable are quick and painless ways to make the unacceptable behavior die out.

Housebreaking

What goes in comes out. Housebreaking is one of the most common sources of dissension, frustration, that the intention is there, so praise is warranted. Even pretty disorganized attempts to comply deserve praise in a young pup.

It's important to grab a pup up even in midstream and cart it to the papers; otherwise, it will decide to hide the mess or do it when you're not looking. Three days of mopping up is, to me, well spent for a lifetime with a dependably housebroken dog. Hit or miss attention to this vital aspect of living together will give you a hit or miss dog, never entirely dependable in the house.

Once Puppy has the paper routine down pat, I move to Step Two. When I see Puppy heading for the paper, I jump up and dash for the door, saying clearly, "Let's go OUT," emphasizing OUT. It may be necessary to carry the puppy outside, but get outside as quickly as possible, before the puppy's urge to eliminate passes.

And yes, you have to be outside, too, rain, cold, night, or whatever. You need to be there for two reasons. The first is that you have to actually *see* the puppy do its business. The second is the matter of praise. Make a big, happy fuss about what a GOOD puppy you have, pat, and then go back into the house. Don't take time for playing now; you're teaching that outside is the place to go for eliminations. Don't dilute a lesson with something that might confuse the pup about why you went out. Make this a simple four step process: 1) Go outside; 2) observe that the puppy eliminates; 3) praise; 4) go back inside. Believe me,

any time you spend in rain or darkness teaching this vital lesson is time well invested. A dependably housebroken dog is a joy to live with.

There are some old, bad suggestions about housebreaking. One of them is that if you find a mess, you rub the pup's nose in it and scold the puppy. This is wrong and dumb. Puppy has forgotten all about making the mess. When you rub its nose in excrement, you display incredibly bad manners, doing something absolutely no dog would ever do to another dog. This is not behavior to teach any dog good habits; all it teaches is that you're a person to be feared—which isn't a lesson you want to teach. Clean up the mess. If it makes you feel better (and it does me) you can exclaim sorrowfully as you clean up about what kind of BAD dog would do such a thing and how disappointed you are. Puppy will not understand one word you're saying, but it will understand your tone and body language. As housebreaking gets more firmly entrenched and as the bond between you and Puppy strengthens, your sorrowful tone will cause Puppy to try harder to please you.

Puppies still in the litter do not mess where they sleep. We've watched really baby puppies stagger off to a corner of the puppy box to eliminate. So as Puppy learns that the house is eating and sleeping quarters, its very nature will help you in your task of housebreaking.

In housebreaking, as in everything else, consistency is important. Use the same commands every time, and insist that everyone else do so, too. Always interrupt if Puppy's going in the wrong place. Always praise good behavior. Every time someone is too lazy to do the right thing, Puppy is taught that the lesson really isn't all that important, and the process will take longer to teach, with the results being less dependable.

Capo di Capi

One of the things that has to be decided among family members is who is the *real* boss, the Big Cheese, the ultimate authority. A pup will accept one alpha dog, but not half a dozen. Hammer this out before Puppy comes home to your house. Then, whoever is the Big Boss decides which commands are to be used, which lessons are vital, what

These puppies know who The Boss is, and they follow along eagerly.

kind of praise—or correction— must be used, and what the schedule is to be. Depending on what breed Puppy is, other family members will fall into place as secondary leaders, siblings, or pieces of the furniture. With our dogs, each puppy seems to choose either Kent or me as alpha; it runs along gender lines, with the dogs looking to me, and the bitches looking to Kent. Jezebel, Kent's favorite bitch, would look at Kent with a "Do I have to?" expression whenever I gave her a command. It took years for her to accept me as a serious leader. Not that she didn't like me, but she had her leader. Now a friend who has a chow is in an entirely different position. Oso, his chow, truly does not care whether another human being exists or not. By nature, the chow is a one-person dog. Some study is indeed warranted before one gets a puppy. Do you want a family dog or an exclusive?

The Right Puppy for You (You Can't Turn a Sow's Ear . . .)

The most understandable reason, to me, for getting a purebred dog is that in each breed, there is a spectrum of behavior or personality traits for which serious breeders have, over the years, selected. This is not to say that every example of that given breed will behave exactly the same way. But with a purebred dog, you have some guidelines, whereas

with a mixed breed, you simply have less to go on. Besides the inbred breed characteristics, every puppy is also influenced by its environment. The age-old question of nature or nurture applies to dogs as well as to people. But there are trends. Therefore, besides choosing one breed over another because you prefer the looks of one, you chose personalities that fit with yours. It's important to learn as much as you can about what to expect of dogs of Puppy's breed, because, as I said before, one of the basic aims of your training is to bring out the best traits of the breed. You can tailor your training to make your puppy a well-behaved example of, say, a weimaraner or a border terrier, knowing the horizons and limitations within which you're working. I am

Pick the puppy that suits your living habits.

assuming that you already have your puppy. If such is not the case, besides this book you need to study the various breed books to see what dog you want.

Sporting Breeds

If, for instance, you have one of the smaller spaniels, like the cockers, you have a puppy who is likely to want to be everybody's friend. These are outgoing dogs who welcome your guests readily. The same is true of most of the sporting breeds—setters, retrievers, pointers. Depending on how widely you socialize puppies of these breeds, you can bring up your puppy to be the Congeniality Kid in any gathering. The sporting dogs are on the go. They suffer from inactivity more than many other dogs. If you're an avid hiker, a sporting dog is for you, because it will delight in your excursions. If, on the other hand, you're a city person, give serious second thoughts to trying to keep a sporting dog happy in the city. Cuddly and sweet though many of them are, sporting dogs tend also to be stubborn, and they are more likely to roam than some other groups of

A six-week-old curly coated retriever.

15

dogs. From what I've listened to over years of being around show dogs and their people, the two breeds most brilliant, inventive, and difficult to train are basenjis and weimaraners. Listening to owners of those two swap war stories might daunt you if you just got a young puppy of either breed. But be of good cheer—you'll never be bored!

Working Breeds

The working breeds, like Welsh corgis, Akitas, rottweilers, Great Danes, and Newfoundlands, tend to be family dogs. Though not averse to strangers, these breeds tend not to care one way or the other whether people outside your family exist. Generally placid and easygoing, the working breeds want to please their family, which makes them relatively easy to train. Training methods appropriate to a sporting dog or a terrier can ruin the temperament of a working dog, changing it from a loyal family protector to a suspicious dog that fears people. Because they guard their home territory, working dogs often fight other dogs on their property. You'll need to be on your

Like all youngsters, rottweiler pups are cuddly and adorable.

guard and not let aggressive behavior begin. Before they are six months old, many large working dogs begin to practice confrontation, especially on other dogs, but sometimes, too, on people. There are some very strong-willed dogs among the working breeds, for all their family loyalty. Be sure you're up to coping with a strong will before deciding to acquire perhaps a rottweiler or a Dane. Some specimens of working dogs have been bred to a more hair-trigger guard mentality than I find I want to live with. Though Dobermans were once considered the epitome of the hyper attack-type dog, in the past 20 years or so Doberman breeders have selected out the quick-to-take-offense dogs in favor of a more restrained type. On the other hand, rottweilers once were mellow family guardians, much like Great Danes, but today I'm seeing more and more rottweilers who are unnecessarily aggressive. A working dog with correct temperament is a fine dog for a family with children but be aware that it needs training.

Hounds

Hounds are of two types: Those that follow their prey by sight, or sighthounds, and those that track their prey by scent. Sighthounds include the Afghan hound, the saluki, and the greyhound. These dogs tend to be introverted and do not demand a lot of attention from their owners. In some ways they're easier to keep in the city than in the country, as they're less likely in the city to spot

prey and take off on 60-mile-an-hour chases. I traveled for several months with a friend and her two sighthounds; during that time I learned the true meaning of the word "aloof," for her dogs were the most self-contained canines I've ever experienced. The hounds that track by scenting their prey include beagles, bloodhounds, and bassets. While some of them can be developed into fine family pets, their nature is to trail game, and they seem unable to resist a fresh scent. Some people thrill to the music of deep hound voices baying on a trail; many neighbors object to such serenades. So if you live in close proximity to others, your hound can't be allowed to stay out late at night and sing to the moon! The two dogs that came closest to driving me crazy were Ralph and George, the beagle brothers. When they weren't out in the yard hunting woodchucks, they'd sit at opposite ends of the house and bark through windows—at each other. More demanding of field time than I wanted, the beagle brothers were much happier when I found them a new home with a man who lived to hunt.

Nonsporting Breeds

A group of dogs curiously dubbed nonsporting are dogs that once had specific jobs to do but who are so attuned to people that they have been made into very favored family pets. Here you'll find such dogs as the schipperke, once the barge dog of the Netherlands, and dalmatians, the legendary fire dogs. Poodles, except the toys, are in this group, as are bulldogs and chows. In this group you'll find dogs that have delighted people for centuries. Close study of the temperament of a given breed here may turn up the ideal dog for you. The chow, for instance, is one of the most loyal and loving dogs in the world, but generally its loyalty is centered on one person.

Many nonsporting dogs take a light training hand because they want to please their owner and learn quickly. If you've ever watched a standard poodle happily going through obedience routines at a dog show, you know how strongly bonded to the wishes of their owners these dogs can be. However, be aware that dalmatians and many

A seven-month-old Irish wolfhound is larger than many full-grown dogs.

In their play, these six-week-old chow puppies are learning important lessons about behavior.

17

bulldogs can be remarkably stubborn, and rare is the chow that responds well to a large family or a situation where strangers are constantly coming and going.

Terriers

If your idea of the ideal dog is one with boundless energy and you happen to have a terrier puppy, you have a match made in heaven. No dogs are so eager to meet life head on as those of the terrier group, nor do many exhibit such joy in life. Here you find the fox, Skye, Kerry blue, and border terriers, among others. These are dogs that live as happily in city as in country, are busy most of the time, and are excellent watchdogs. Their one drawback is that they tend to be noisy, so your training needs to include lessons on what needs to be barked at and what doesn't. The big terriers such as Airedales are very territorial; like working dogs, their aggressiveness toward other dogs needs to be curbed. The same is true for Staffordshire terriers.

Toy Breeds

For the person who wants a small personal pet, looking to the toy group is advisable. Here you'll find many breeds that are small scale replicas of either larger breeds or former breeds, as well as dogs that were deliberately developed for small spaces. The pug, the papillon, and the Pekingese, for instance, are excellent choices for the person who wants a happy little dog that can thrive in an apartment, can get plenty of exercise chasing a ball around the house, and who will cheerfully spend lots of time on a lap. It's thought that Pekingese were originally bred to keep people's arms warm in drafty old Chinese castles. The dogs were known as "sleeve dogs." The toy dogs aren't ideal for small children, however; as puppies, they're tiny and fragile. Some of the toys are given to yapping, so if you have a toy, be vigilant in teaching your pup to be quiet when you tell it to be. Toys need not be yappy, snappish, or neurotic. My friend Gene raises Chihuahuas, and I delight in watching him set off on his round of farm chores trailed by a happy pack of busy little Chihuahuas, none of

whom exhibit the negative behaviors so many people associate with that breed. But Gene treats his Chihuahuas as dogs, not windup toys, which I think is the secret to well-mannered toy dogs.

Herding Breeds

In recent years some of the working group have been split off to form the herding group. Here you'll find German shepherds, collies, Old English sheepdogs, and the like. Many of these dogs have the basic temperament of the working dogs, but overlaid on this is their natural tendency to herd. And herd they will, often keeping busy until they have their family all neatly gathered in one room! Some of the more heavily coated herding dogs are uncomfortable in the house. Alaskan malamutes and Siberian huskies fall into this category. Their herding and sledding instincts are still close to the surface, and they fare far better doing what they were bred for than lying around as house pets.

People have bred dogs for centuries, carefully selecting for some traits and suppressing others. Some breedings have been more successful than others in producing dogs that adjust to close living with people. You'll notice, for instance, that I have not mentioned coonhounds or cattle dogs as house pets. While these dogs are perfect for what they were bred to do, they aren't bred to live in daily house proximity to people. For the dog lover, there is the perfect breed for each person's idiosyncratic needs. If you find that you inadver-

Though resting quietly, this German shepherd puppy is keenly aware of its surroundings.

tently acquired a puppy of a breed that does not fit your temperament, consult seriously with the breeder who sold you the puppy. Most ethical breeders would rather take a puppy back than have it in a home where no one's going to be really happy.

No matter what breed you settle on—or what breed adopts you—there is one truth all of us have to bear in mind: Puppies grow up to be dogs. Every puppy is an immature dog. They are not miniature people or substitute children. Their understanding is a dog's understanding, as their instincts are dogs' instincts. I have met all too many people who seem unable to grasp this basic concept and who harbor ill-mannered, untrained dogs that drive everyone crazy. Many of these dogs eventually either get passed from family to family or end up in animal shelters, where they are finally killed because they are not fit to live with human beings.

Correction, Not Cruelty

The uncorrected puppy grows up to be an uncivil dog. My mother had

Don't be fooled by this puppy's sad look— bassets are fun-loving dogs.

a series of unmannerly poodles because she would never correct them. Her usual response to anything a dog did was to say, "Oh, don't scold him!" So her dogs piddled on the rugs, growled at her when she had to give them medication, and bit her when she tried to brush or bathe them.

They did none of those things to me.

Every dog grows up knowing exactly how far they can push each human around them.

Throughout this book, I'm sharing scams I've learned from puppies and dogs that block, derail, or change unwanted behavior. At no time am I going to advise you to beat your dog, rub its nose in excrement, chain it in a corner of the yard, or in any way be cruel to it. In fact, just the other day I stepped up to a man who was hitting his dog and said, "You stop that this very

minute!" The man was so furious he could scarcely speak, and for a minute I thought I was going to be the next victim of his heavy hand.

"You don't even know what I was doing!" he yelled at me. "This dog won't walk on a leash."

"May I?" I asked, reaching out my hand for the pup's leash.

A little coaxing, a little jollying, lots of "That's a GOOD puppy," and the pup was trotting along, wagging his tail as if he'd known all along how to walk on a leash. I do hope his owner could see the difference.

Yes, there's altogether too much cruelty to puppies—and to children, too—when it comes to lessons. And that cruelty doesn't accomplish anything positive.

What I'm about here is a positive, humane way to bring a puppy or older dog around to the point where it's a happy animal and a welcome member of its human family. This, I've found over many years of living with dogs and puppies, is far preferable to letting the puppy do what it wants, no matter how unlikely it is that such behavior will make it welcome in the world of people.

Domesticated. Civilized. That's the kind of puppies most folks want to live with.

Prepare, Prepare!

Most of us work outside our homes. So, unlike the good old days of nostalgia, in most homes a puppy has to spend hours alone. I've noticed that often people overlook the reality of that first day that they have to go to work after buying a new puppy. Then, in the helter-skelter of getting ready to go to the job, there arises the question, "What happens to this puppy all day?" You can't crate a puppy all day—that's cruel. You can't give a new puppy run of the house—that's asking for devastation, and it's potentially dangerous for the puppy, too. Nor can you expect a young pup to be continent for nine or more hours. So who walks it or lets it out for potty runs?

Ideally you get a new pup when you have a few days free for early training and socializing. But maybe you have only a weekend. Whatever time you have, figure out what facilities you need in order for that puppy to flourish when you have to go away. You may have to do some fast construction to create a pen and warm sleeping quarters. Maybe you'll have to modify a room in your apartment for a puppy's safety. But get done whatever you need to do before that first day of separation. Otherwise, whatever good first steps you've taken will be undercut by perhaps a ruined carpet when you get home, or a puppy that hanged itself on a tie-out chain or neighbors banging on your door to complain about the puppy crying all day.

I think that if I were going to start a new business, I'd open a day care center for puppies! Given the number of hours that people work and the amount of idle, lonely time many puppies are forced to deal with, day care sounds like a winner to me!

But since I'm not starting a new business just now, let me ask you seriously—is this a time in your life when you really have the resources to deal with a new puppy? The time? The patience? The right living quarters? The stability? I know there's no love like wriggly, warm puppy love, but the people have to hold up their end of the bargain, too. I have a friend we'll call Jane who did, indeed, create a fine, comfortable place for her poodle during work hours. However, given the demands of Jane's job, she's away from home often ten hours a day. Guess what? Even when Jane's at home, the poodle prefers her outside quarters to being in the house, even to the point that she no longer wants to sleep inside at night. This was not what Jane had in mind when she got her dog, but it's what happens when a dog is forced to depend on its own devices for too many hours in a day.

On the other end of the spectrum, I've noticed many retired folks with recreational vehicles traveling with happy, well-adjusted dogs. These people have the time to share with their pets, because the demands of upward mobility no longer drain their time and energies.

Part of preparing for a puppy is determining realistically whether you are going to give that puppy the time it needs—and deserves.

Chapter 2

You, Your Pup, and Your Veterinarian

After you and the rest of your immediate family, the next person your puppy needs to get to know is your veterinarian. If you're as fortunate as I've been, you'll find a veterinarian whose help, advice, and teaching will make you easily able to handle whatever health emergencies arise with your new puppy. The ideal is that you and the vet you choose will become a team. After you, the veterinarian is your puppy's best friend—if you do your job right and

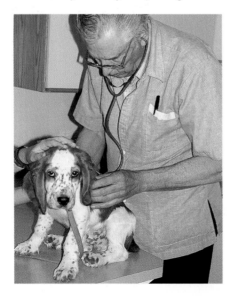

Next to you, a caring, able veterinarian is your dog's best friend.

choose a knowledgeable, caring, communicative vet who puts pets first. I've found in general that veterinarians have been more forthcoming with health information than people doctors are. With some exceptions, they're fully committed to the well-being of their four-footed patients, even if it means they have to be firm with the patient's owner. I think here of Dr. John Carricaburu, who got pretty hot when he was talking about people who refused to feed their dogs healthful diets.

"People come in with poor, fat, sickly little poodles," he said to me. "The dogs have rotten teeth, scruffy coats, and obvious signs of malnutrition. I ask what they're feeding the dog, and they tell me, 'Oh, he eats just what I eat.' Then I blow up and tell them, 'He's a dog. Feed him what a dog needs."

Dr. John admitted that many times he failed to get the message across. "But I keep trying," he said. "For the good of the dogs, I have to try."

The best veterinarians are passionate in their concern for their patients, and that's the kind of vet I recommend you find. They'll also spend generous explaining time with you, because your understanding is vital to Puppy's good health.

An Ounce of Prevention

Within 24 hours of getting your puppy, take it to your vet. A conscientious breeder will ask that you do this to double-check that Puppy is healthy. If the breeder is local, s/he'll probably suggest that you use the same vet Puppy has already been seeing. If not, ask friends whom they use; if you had a vet you liked for your Dear Departed old dog, then you already have a vet you trust.

Even if Puppy seems entirely healthy, has had first shots, and everything's going just fine, still make that initial visit. You want to make sure Puppy isn't incubating something exotic and unique to your area, for even though ethical breeders will replace sick pups, after 48 hours they are understandably uneasy about returning to the litter a puppy that might have picked up some strange disease from another area. Besides, if some problem is brewing, you want to deal with it as soon as possible. If there's no problem, then your vet gets to see Puppy as a well dog and has a benchmark for that particular dog.

Bring a sample of the puppy's feces with you when you visit the veterinarian. Use a plastic bag or a small disposable container to carry this. The vet will want it to test for internal parasites, like worms.

Be Positive

This first trip to the vet's is your chance to do some good early training. Puppy needs to learn that trips to the vet are fun times, to be looked forward to. So keep your attitude enthusiastic and your voice cheerful and confident. I was amazed to get a call from my friend Betty telling me that Bambi, her pushy Dane bitch puppy, fell apart at the vet's and had to be dragged into the examining room. Wanting to see for myself what was making an otherwise well-socialized puppy terrified in the vet's office, I hid myself in a small alcove where I could observe the waiting room when Betty and Bambi were due.

In they came, Bambi cowering on leash, and Betty commiserating with her in tones that told the puppy how awful, scary, and dangerous this whole trip was. "Poor Bambi!" Betty repeated, stroking her head, "It'll be all right. I'll be right there."

"'Poor Bambi,' my foot!" I announced, taking the leash. "Come on, Bambi," I said in my most cheerful voice, patting her vigorously, "we're going to visit your doctor!" The words were unimportant. The tone and my firm assurance were what mattered. Bambi perked up, cast a last glance at Betty, and trotted willingly into the examining room. It was a routine booster-shot trip, and I jollied her along for the few moments of the procedure, then hustled her out through the waiting room, proclaiming what a good time she'd had on this outing.

Betty quickly realized that her tone and body language were communicating danger and threat to Bambi, and, as she was devoted to making Bambi's life a good one, she changed her approach to trips to the vet's. Never again did she have to drag a cowering Bambi into a vet's office.

So. Your attitude and body language are the key here. Realizing that the vet is your puppy's friend will help you be positive about the trip. Puppy can tell from how tense or relaxed you are whether a situation is a threat or a treat.

Proper Control at the Vet's

If Puppy is still tiny, not leash-trained, and unprotected by any immunizations, carry him or her all the way. Most dogs that go to the vet's are sick, and no matter how spick-and-span the staff keep a waiting room, your pup is better off not walking through whatever germs may be present. If Puppy is leash-trained (or too big to carry), keep her or him away from other dogs in the waiting room. This isn't a social situation. Other dogs may be sick, aren't feeling well, and don't want to be bothered by a bouncy

puppy. And you don't want other dogs' germs! Be equally firm about insisting that other waiting owners keep their dogs away from Puppy. For years I've deplored the insensitivity of people in vets' waiting rooms, many bursting in with some lout of a dog not on leash and under no control.

The Physical

This first physical will let you know how Puppy is doing overall. The doctor will do the routine things—listen to Puppy's heart, check its temperature, go over its teeth and gums, check sight and hearing, and examine it for general soundness. The fecal sample will tell whether internal parasites like worms are present, and, depending on Puppy's age, blood may be drawn to check on internal parasites that don't show up in feces. This is a good time to ask about what specific things you should watch for in your puppy's breed. You may also ask about your puppy's diet, as well as what to look for in proper growth and development.

Such factors as coat condition and skin tone will let the vet know whether Puppy is getting the right diet. The doctor will look to see whether the puppy teeth are falling out properly. Sometimes one or two stay in too long and block the adult tooth from coming in normally. In that case, the vet may pull the retained baby teeth. If your pup is getting adult teeth by now, this is the time to learn how to brush your dog's teeth. I'd been skeptical about brushing a dog's teeth, believing the old stories about biscuits and bones and proper diet taking all the care a dog's teeth need. But when I was writing *Caring for Older Cats & Dogs,* my coauthor, Dr. Robert Anderson, convinced me beyond any doubt that starting a puppy off right includes dental hygiene.

"What happens to a dog that has decayed teeth and the poisons from tooth decay leach into its system year in and year out?" Bob asked me. "How healthy can it be, no matter what you feed it?"

Well, that makes sense to me. More and more I hear about older dogs that seem to get a new lease on life after they have rotten teeth pulled. So my next new puppy will learn to have its teeth brushed. I recommend the process to you, too. Ask your vet to show you how to brush a puppy's teeth, and purchase the correct cleaning compound and brush before you leave.

External Parasites

If you're wondering why I include a discussion of parasites and their control in a book mainly about civilizing your new puppy, this is the reason: Anything that interferes with your pup's health also interferes with your training program. Heavy or persistent infestations of external or internal parasites drag your puppy's health down. A chronically sickly puppy not only doesn't flourish, it also doesn't learn well. Thus, coping with parasites is a major step in making sure your puppy is ready and able to concentrate on learning important lessons in civilized puppy behavior.

Depending on where you live, your puppy will be plagued by some array of fleas, ticks, and mites. Year in and year out we wage war on these plagues. The chemical arsenal is vast; however, when we use poisons to kill any parasites, we're also introducing some level of toxicity into our puppy's system. I am firmly in the camp that believes in using the least harsh, least intrusive poisons and still get the job done. That said, let's look at what your vet might suggest for Puppy.

Fleas

For fleas and ticks, the pyrethrum-based powders and sprays are the least toxic to the puppy. These products don't have a long span of effectiveness, so you have to use them frequently. Their plus factor is that they're less harmful to your pup than most other parasite controls, so even

An adult flea, magnified.

frequent dustings or sprayings are not loading your pup's system with poison. Excessive dosing should still be avoided, of course. Be sure to follow your vet's recommendations or those on the package of the product.

Last year, under our vet's guidance, Kent and I went on a crusade against fleas before our dogs started scratching, using products that stop flea eggs from hatching. We spent a month conscientiously treating the house, the kennel, and the dogs themselves with flea killers containing the preemergent chemical known as Precor. That month was time well invested, let me tell you. Never before had we had no further trouble with fleas, though where we live is truly Flea Heaven as far as climate is concerned. This spring we again went through everything, and again we're ahead of the game. Best of all, our dogs aren't having to cope with harsh chemicals, for the product we're using is lethal to the fleas and their eggs, not to the dogs.

Flea collars are common and popular, but not with me and not with many vets who lean toward reducing the chemical load on a dog's system. On a baby puppy, if you hang a flea collar around its neck, you're sentencing it to 24 hours of breathing in poisonous fumes, as well as having some toxic substance constantly rubbing on its neck. Any flea with a grain of sense, however, is cavorting around back by Puppy's tail, totally unaffected by the toxic fumes. So where's the gain? And by the time your giant puppy grows up—say into a St. Bernard—how much good is a little strip of poison around its neck really going to do to the world of fleas on its body? Even more toxic are the flea collars saturated with chemicals that your pup absorbs through its skin.

I've found one good use for flea collars, though. Before we rid the house of fleas, I cut up a new flea collar and put it in the vacuum cleaner bag. At least the fleas trapped in there die.

Organophosphates are the next step up from the pyrethums in toxicity. Perhaps on an older puppy that's heavily infested with fleas, you'll need to use one of these products until you knock down the flea population. Work with your vet, though, on a program that's going to rid your part of the world of fleas—as we did—in such a way that Puppy isn't going to have to fight against a chemical load all the time.

The subject of chemical load brings us to a consideration of some parasite controllers that are taken internally. Some are injected, and some are in capsule form. Proponents of both kinds claim they are superior to other flea controls because they cause any flea that bites the treated dog to die. People like me question whether flea control warrants introducing chemicals into my dogs' systems when I can achieve the same result—perhaps with a little more trouble—by treating the dog and our living quarters externally.

That said, it's important to look at some new developments in the internal control of external parasites. The new Program product, which is similar to Precor in its action, is quite safe. This is another product that is available from your veterinarian. One of my favorite veterinarians once said to me, "Every year the parasites become more resistant to the chemicals we've been using to kill them, but fortunately, every year, veterinary scientists come up with something better, so we stay ahead of the game." With our increasing awareness that chemicals need to be carefully evaluated for side effects, it appears that scientists are developing what one might call more environmentally friendly products for parasite control.

Probably the most important point I want to make here is that you need to discuss these matters with your veterinarian, not with a pet store clerk! Go to the pet store for food, toys, beds, combs, and such, but when it's a matter of your puppy's health, go to the trained professional.

Ticks

Because Lyme disease has so recently made the headlines, we're all more aware than before of the dangers posed by ticks. No one knows yet how extensive Lyme disease is in dogs, but all of us want to minimize our pets' risk of being infected. A vaccine against Lyme disease for dogs is on the market. It's new so we don't yet have extensive studies to show how effective it is over time. However, its success

rate is between 80 to 90 percent. It can't be used on puppies before 12 weeks of age. Then it needs to be repeated in another few weeks and annually boosted. Dr. Chuck Ozanian, a veterinarian in Ferndale, California, tells me that some vets at the Veterinary School at Davis report seeing negative side effects, though he hasn't seen any yet. Side effects are proving to be extremely rare.

Even if you don't live in a Lyme disease hot spot, use all reasonable methods to control ticks. Most pyrethrin-based flea products are effective in preventing tick attachment. There are also sprays containing DEET; however, these are harsh and of questionable safety.

Brushing Puppy after an outing in the fields or woods is important; you'll perhaps find ticks, and you'll be likely to brush off ticks that haven't yet attached themselves. The more heavily coated your puppy is, the more attentive you'll have to be, getting down to the skin and looking for ticks.

If you find a tick, forget the old stuff we used to think was right— daubing on grease to make the tick back out, using something hot to kill the tick, and so forth. Pull the tick

A tick before feeding (left), and after feeding (right).

straight out carefully but with a firm pressure. Using tweezers or wearing gloves is a good precaution. Not every tick carries Lyme disease, and not every bite results in infection. But Lyme disease is serious enough that we all need to keep our dogs as free of ticks as we can without blighting their lives!

Mites

The most common mites we see on dogs are ear mites. Especially if you have indoor/outdoor cats, the chances are good that Puppy may pick up ear mites. Your vet will check for these on the initial physical and tell you what to do to get rid of them. If at any time you see Puppy shaking its ears and digging at them, have it checked for ear mites. Control is fairly easy, though you must be persistent.

Not Over the Counter

I've consistently referred to products your vet will advise to control parasites—both internal and external. Because all products for para-

site control depend for their results on poisoning the parasites, they're all more or less toxic and hence more or less hazardous to your pet. Any vet you trust enough to treat Puppy will keep current on what products are most effective in controlling parasites with the least harm. Vets have access to products that aren't sold over the counter, and, generally speaking, you can trust what the vet suggests. Furthermore, should Puppy have a negative reaction to a product your vet has suggested, the vet will know how to counteract that reaction.

Internal Parasites

Once at a dog show I saw an enormous jar filled with all the worms that had, allegedly, been removed from one dog. The sight sickened me, but obviously it was an effective advertisement, for I've remembered it. It's true that a disgusting array of worms can infest puppies, from roundworms, tapeworms, and heartworms to whipworms and wireworms. Some are easier to get rid of than others. Some are quickly life-threatening, while others hang on and sap your pup's health and vitality, killing it by inches.

Your vet is the one who will diagnose and prescribe for whatever worms Puppy may have, now or in the future. Sometimes it's a onetime deal and the worms are gone. Other

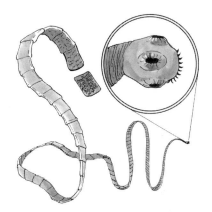

A tapeworm, with a close-up of the head.

times, as with heartworms, which are becoming more widely dispersed across the country, lifelong preventive control is essential. Even more than with external parasites, these internal ones need to be purged by your knowledgeable, caring vet. Don't fool around self-diagnosing and using broad-spectrum poisons available over the counter.

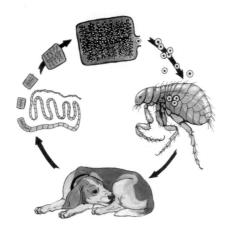

Fleas are significant in the life cycle of tapeworms. As intermediate hosts, they carry the parasite's eggs to dogs.

Immunizations

When I was a child, puppy ads often advised, "Has had distemper." This was the bane of the canine world; many pups died of it, and the survivors were highly prized. Today, veterinary science has gifted us with a marvelous array of vaccines that give puppies a very high rate of immunity from diseases. Though there are occasional negative reactions and the odd puppy that doesn't get high immunity, for the most part, a properly immunized puppy stands a fine chance of growing up to be a healthy dog. Bearing in mind my bias toward the least intrusive methods that are consistent with good results, talk with your vet on your first visit about what immunizations Puppy needs. If Puppy has already had some shots, bring the record of exactly what product was used. It's important to know what was used and when, for many vaccines depend on a time factor for optimum effectiveness.

The basic immunization right now is referred to as a DHLPP. That refers

to distemper, hepatitis, leptospirosis, parvovirus, and parainfluenza. This series is repeated at intervals in about an 8-week span, usually starting at 8 weeks, then again at 12 and 16 weeks. Then you plan the annual booster shots. Your vet will tell you if other common diseases in your area dictate routine immunization. At some point there'll also be a rabies shot, and states have individual laws about how often this is boosted. The basic immunizations are protection against each common disease that is more or less life-threatening to a

Proper immunizations are vital to a puppy's health.

And again, let me emphasize that this isn't the time to get chintzy and buy over-the-counter stuff! Immunization is serious business, insurance that will influence a lifetime.

Spaying or Neutering

This first trip isn't too soon to discuss the pros and cons of spaying or neutering your puppy. Your vet will tell you the best time to do the operation, should you so decide. Unless you are serious about the breeding of dogs and your puppy is an excellent breeding candidate, spaying or neutering is a wise choice. You can discuss any behavior changes that might occur, such as less tendency to roam in the dog that's neutered. There are many myths about what spaying or neutering does and doesn't do to a dog, and no one can dispel those myths better than a knowledgeable vet.

puppy. We're not talking exotic stuff here; this isn't the time to knock your puppy's system for a loop with every vaccine known to science! Done properly, the basic immunizations aren't going to have negative side effects. However, ask your vet what are the possible signs of a negative reaction. Best to be able to observe with knowledge than to worry.

If, on the other hand, yours is a puppy that's a valuable part of a breeding program, your vet's guidance on diet and care will be good to have right from the start.

Tattooing

One of the most foolproof ways to identify your puppy is to have it tattooed. The various tattoo registries have splendid records of returning lost or stolen dogs to their owners. A

tattoo is permanent; unlike an identification tag on a collar, it can't simply be tossed away. Your vet, who is likely to be part of a tattoo registry, can advise you how early a puppy can be tattooed. Many veterinarians do the tattooing themselves. In some areas, the local humane society sponsors tattooing clinics.

Beyond the tattoo are the new microchip implants, possibly the wave of the future in dog identification. Inserted with a hypodermic needle under the dog's skin, this wonderful product of our new electronic age is a quick, painless, permanent way to record who your dog is and where s/he belongs.

Learn to Communicate

No matter how brilliant your puppy is, s/he will never be able to tell the vet what's wrong. That is your job—you're the interpreter. In your initial visit to your chosen vet, find out how well the two of you humans communicate. You don't have to be a whiz at veterinary medicine to ask a vet what to watch for if Puppy's having a bad reaction to immunizations, for instance. And a caring vet can explain to you in clear language.

Any veterinarian who is unwilling to explain, who talks to you in jargon you can't understand, or who acts as if you're intruding when you want explanations should be immediately crossed off your list as a partner in your puppy's health care. All the sci-entific expertise in the world is useless if the doctor is unwilling to collaborate with you, the person most involved in Puppy's life. If you don't know what to do, treatment, most of which takes place at home, isn't going to be optimum.

Your part in this continuing dialogue is to report as clearly, accurately, and specifically as possible. Write down questions you want to ask the vet before you leave home. Dr. John taught me to keep records when Heidi was having her first litter. Ever after, when a dog begins showing signs that all isn't well, I start jotting down my perceptions—a record of exactly what happened and when it happened. The doctor can tell a lot from such specifics, like whether a condition is getting worse, stabilized, or on the wane. Not only that, but we all tend to get more or less frightened when our dog is in crisis, and the written record can take the place of our wits, which may have deserted us. It's not helpful to have a person saying, "I think it was yesterday . . . no, maybe it was the day before." Your organization and clear information are vitally helpful.

Don't be afraid to ask, but likewise, don't be careless with the information you're given. Jot down notes about what the vet tells you, so that later you're not depending on a faulty memory.

What Can You Do?

As a partner in your dog's health care, find out how much you can and can't do to assist your vet

taught my husband and me a great deal about recognizing emergencies early, before they've gone beyond help. That we've been fortunate in finding excellent veterinarians willing to teach us has made a positive difference in our dogs' long and healthy lives, as well as in our confidence that we can do well by our dogs. Everyone, I think, who cares about a pet wants this kind of rapport with their dog's other best friend.

Not a Crowd Scene

Sometimes it's tough to find someone to watch children if you have an emergency trip to the vet's, but insofar as is possible, remember that such a trip is for Puppy, not the kids. If you're distracted by other family members who can't be part of the solution to the immediate problem, you're not going to listen as well as you must to instructions and explanations. A sick or hurt dog needs as calm an atmosphere as possible, yet children are likely to be very upset if their pet is hurt. Even the doctor may be distracted by clamoring children. Everybody loses.

during a visit. Can you hold Puppy still for shots? Is Puppy dependable about not snapping? Can you hold his/her head so the vet is safe? If you're comfortable as an assistant, your dog will appreciate your presence. But if you fall apart when Puppy is ill, recognize that fact, because your agitation is going to transmit directly to your pup, making a tense situation worse. You need to be able to say, "I'm not much good in this situation, and I'd better leave." Far from thinking less of you, your vet and the staff will be glad of your honesty.

Kent and I have assisted at some late and touchy times, mostly with George. He was a teacher par excellence and quick to tell either of us what to do. Being able to assist during our dogs' emergencies has

Promise the children that you'll report everything when you get home. Perhaps if you have an older child who is especially good with Puppy, that child might come along to help in the car. But keep the priorities clear: Emergency trips are not crowd scenes!

Chapter 3

Essential Equipment

The items you'll come to regard as essential for living happily with your puppy fall into four basic categories: control, comfort, fun, and grooming. You can, if you choose, spend a small fortune on these, but I'll deal with the basics—what you really need and why you need it. We all like the occasional frill, and we all suit our own taste in the frills department. It's only necessary to be sure the frills are also safe.

Control

Collars
Puppy will grow through several collars, so don't buy the most expensive models for each interim stage. However, plan on having two different kinds for each stage of Puppy's development.

The choker, or choke collar, gives you maximum control over an exuberant, bouncing puppy just learning manners. I prefer to begin with a nylon or cotton webbing choker, which is at least half an inch (1.3 cm) wide and sturdy. The reason for this preference is that the webbing is softer than a chain collar on the

puppy's neck and seems to frighten a puppy less. You still have good control, for all chokers tighten up when a pup pulls and release when it heels along in the proper position and at your set pace. My experience has been that at some time about seven or eight months of age, big puppies can use a bit more snappy reminder of what they're supposed to be doing than the webbing, or soft, choker gives. I change then to a heavier chain choker. The big, heavy links don't cut the puppy's

"Just get me the essentials!"

Top: Necessary collars— a chain choker (left), and a strap collar (right). Bottom: The correct way to put a choker on.

neck as the thinner chains generally used in show rings do, and they give you all the force you need to correct a big, strong puppy. I forgot to leash-train Cappy, that big funny lout of a Dane, until he was almost a year old. We lived in a very remote country place, and a leash wasn't necessary for the walks we took in the woods with his mother and Starbuck, my weimaraner.

But suddenly it was time to begin Cappy's show career, and here I had a really big puppy who had no idea what collars and leashes were all about. I bought the strongest chain choker I could, snapped onto it the six-foot leather leash that I'd used for years, and did my first leash-

training lesson. Three times Cappy lunged to the end of the leash, straining that collar to its maximum. Three times I dug in my heels and let him dump himself when he didn't come when called. The fourth time, Cappy gave me a quizzical look, trotted over to me and stood waiting, his entire body language asking, "Is this what you had in mind?" From then on, he knew that wearing this chain choker meant that he had to pay attention to my commands. Your puppy will, indeed, quickly learn that a certain collar means it has to behave in a particular way.

In a very few months, Cappy was ready for the kind of choker I like to use on adult dogs—a round, corded nylon one. For the show ring, I chose black, as it didn't break the lovely line of his neck. Considerations like this are important when looks matter at least as much as utility. Nor does one have to be showing a puppy to be concerned about looks! However, don't forget practicality, too. The corded choker is soft, yet strong enough that a trained adult dog knows it's still time to tend to business.

I used to believe that there is never a situation in which a person would need a prong or pinch collar, and I categorically claim that such a collar is unnecessary for a small puppy. However, I've seen instances where a large adult dog has been allowed to dominate his owner for too long and is out of hand. A prong collar in such situations is a tool for getting the unruly dog's prompt attention. Since the pinching action of the collar depends on the dog's behavior, any dog with half a brain quickly learns to listen to the owner's commands and thus avoid being pinched by the collar. In a matter of a few training sessions, the prong collar becomes unnecessary—a regular chain choker will suffice.

So, as a temporary tool in a drastic situation, I have come to accept the usefulness of prong collars. The alternatives, like not being able to take your dog out anywhere in public, or consigning a dog to the pound, are far less acceptable, I think, than a few training sessions that will get the dog's attention.

The strap collar is the other kind you'll want to have around. The nylon webbing ones are the least expensive. Perhaps when Puppy is an adult you may want to spring for a leather collar, as there are some very handsome ones available. The strap collar is the one a puppy or dog wears just hanging out in the house or yard, or perhaps later, in the field. A well-trained adult dog can also go on walks wearing a strap collar, though you have to be aware that you don't have the control of a choker. Many a dog has adeptly drawn its head back and slipped out of a strap collar.

Never leave a choker on a puppy or a dog that is either unattended, or out in the field, or in a crate. You know haunting panic if you watch your field dog leap a stone wall, get his choker caught on a low-hanging branch, and dangle, kicking and choking in midair. I was lucky because I was in the woods with Blitz when this happened and was able to get my shoulders under him and tear off the tree limb. Not only did that choker come off his neck almost as soon as his feet touched the ground; I never since have gone into the field with any dog wearing anything except an easily slipped strap collar. I'm not the only person to experience such terror. As I said, I'm luckier than others who have come home to dogs that had been hanged on fences or overhanging trees.

Finally, there are various electronic and battery-powered shock collars. One must be extremely careful in ever using these. For instance, Deckrosh, who bred boxers and had a boarding kennel, bought a shock collar to condition dogs who barked incessantly when they were kenneled. He tested the collar on a Sunday and found it effective in controlling a big German shepherd. However, using the same collar on the same dog the next day, he found that the dog shrieked in pain when he applied the shock. When he explored the cause, he discovered that any electronic impulses for up to five miles away would go through the collar, increasing the jolt to perhaps lethal levels. On Sunday, the X-ray department in the hospital across the street from Deckrosh was closed, but on Monday, when it was operating, the collar became too dangerous to use. He abandoned it, as there was never any way to know what kinds of impulses might be added to the collar's own level of shock. Under his guidance, we bought a much simpler collar that is battery-powered and buzzes mildly when a dog barks. We tested it on ourselves many times before deciding that it was mild enough to use on one of our dogs that was driving the neighbors crazy with barking. We've since loaned it to others and found it safe and effective, but we use it only in extreme cases.

Leashes

The standard training leash is a stout 6-foot (2 m) strap with a strong clasp. Again, nylon or cotton webbing is less expensive than leather, though leather lasts forever. I have a 30-year-old leather leash that is just lovely from all the years of handling, and it's just as strong as it was the day I bought it. Pay good attention to the clasp, because that's what takes the strain of a puppy like Cappy who's trying to make a beeline for the horizon. Cheap clasps have

caused many a puppy owner grief in the form of a disappearing pup.

Start right from the beginning and don't let Puppy play with the leash. It's not a toy, and chewing on it is a bad habit to be broken immediately. Swat Puppy with your hand smartly under the chin and say NO very definitely. Swatting under the chin is important. For some reason, dogs don't associate such a swat with the human hand and hence do not become hand-shy as dogs who are swatted on the nose do.

Though I'll consistently tell you how to break bad habits before they become entrenched, I am not going to give you all the standard obedience routines like heeling and so forth. There are very good reasons for me not to, including the fact that there are already excellent obedience books on the market (see page 106). Second, most of the frantic phone calls I've gotten have nothing to do with the standard obedience courses, yet these are the problems that make living with a puppy impossible until they're solved. Third, and maybe the most important, the kinds of behavior that I'm helping you avoid or correct are the problems that too often result in a puppy's being taken to a dog pound, where 60–80 percent of the dogs do not find new homes and are finally killed. However, because many books don't deal adequately with how to begin leash-training with an 8-to-12-week-old puppy, in Chapter 4, I'll tell you the method I've found most effective.

Remember: a leash is not a toy.

Do not buy a chain leash. Contrary to appearances, chains don't give you as much control as straps do. There's that one inadequate padded hand-hold; if you try to hold any other part of a chain leash to snap it and get control of your puppy, you'll hurt your hand. Furthermore, the clatter of the chain spooks many pups.

A leash that's very handy is an all-in-one choker and leash, often made of nylon and available in leather. It's useful for well trained adult dogs, often used in lieu of a leash-choker combination in the show ring, and nice for early training lessons for very young puppies who aren't going to able to give you all that much tugging.

Because the size of the choker is adjustable, it's handy to have for a growing pup or if you have more than one dog. But be aware that these aren't especially strong, and you don't have that much control. Many kennels use a much stronger version of this, the come-along, made of nylon webbing and useful because one size fits all.

A more recent arrival on the market is a retractable leash in a sturdy plastic housing. This outfit can be used as a short leash in traffic or crowded situations and then reeled out to its full 15 or 20 feet (5–7 m) in the field or on walks in uncrowded situations.

Finally, there's the lunge line, a light, long, extremely strong piece of equipment with an excellent clasp that's used to control incorrigible

The retractable leash is ideal in many situations.

dogs who run as soon as they think they're off leash. It's unlikely you'll need this if you start right, but if you, like friends of ours, rescue a dog who is a runner, knowing about this and using it could save a dog's life. Let the dog run the length of the lunge line and call it to come. When it doesn't, plant yourself firmly, dig in your heels, hang on to the line, and dump the would-be runaway. Since the dog thought it was free, this correction comes as a shock and gets its attention. One minute the dog thought it was free, and the next, it's on its back, still under your bidding. A session or two of such training goes a long way to persuade the uncooperative or stubborn dog of your omnipotence. Since this is a test of dominance, or alpha status, it also carries over into other training situations, because the dog is learning that you are, in fact, the leader of the pack. Use of the lunge line should never be mistaken as a substitute for proper early leash training, nor, in fact, have I ever needed to use such training. However, I've watched others reclaim utterly

There are any number of bed styles available. Make sure the one you select is large enough for puppy to grow into.

out-of-control dogs with the method. It's one of those pieces of information you might need sometime in your life.

Comfort

Beds

First in the comfort department is a comfortable bed. The bigger the dog, the more cushiony the bed needs to be. You've perhaps seen older dogs with big, bare patches on their elbows. These come from lying on hard, unyielding surfaces. So start a big puppy, especially, with lots of bed. Once again, don't spend big money for a puppy's bed, because Puppy will undoubtedly chew part or all of it. If you've got a fine dog bed saved from your Dear Departed, put it away safely until Puppy is old enough to be trusted with it! For the meantime, visit secondhand stores and get some inexpensive blankets that will do just

fine. Once we could find inexpensive cot mattresses at such stores, and they're wonderful, but good buys are rare now.

As I indicated earlier when discussing where to have Puppy sleep the first few nights, every puppy will find and adopt its own place in your house. You can expedite the process by making up a box for a young puppy with its bedding in it and placing the bed/box where you want Puppy to sleep. Very soon Puppy will understand "Go to bed" and make a beeline for her/his spot. Most dogs learn to go to bed when their family does. Like all other habits, bedtime becomes an expected event, and the resident dog doesn't understand when guests stay late at night! Their training and expectations say it's bedtime, yet here you are, not making the usual moves. Everyone who has lived closely with dogs in their families has some amusing and embarrassing stories to tell about older dogs who insist on letting the guests know that it's bedtime and would they please go home. Judy, our parti-colored cocker with whom I grew up, would go partway up the stairs, sit, and sigh loudly when she thought it was time for bed. Killer used to embarrass us with guests by sneaking up on his couch in the living room no matter who was sitting on it, get behind them, and then stretch out and kick, giving loud, disgusted groans as he tried to get comfortable. No one could fail to notice, and when they asked what was wrong, one of us would have to admit that it was past his bedtime. Friends had a Bouvier who regularly rounded them up and tried to herd them off to bed if they stayed up too late on weekends.

The Crate

Unless you've been actively showing a dog, traveling long distances, and perhaps sending your dog off with a handler, you may not be used to thinking in terms of having a crate for your dog. Now, with a new puppy, you'd be doing yourself a favor to consider acquiring a crate (also known as a kennel). In the simplest terms, a crate is a glorified box. Thus, when you were teaching your very young puppy to go to its box, you were preparing it for its crate later on. There is, in fact, no reason why you can't, if you prefer, start off right away with the crate and skip the box-training step. A crate can be made of wood, plastic, or wire. It is totally enclosed, with a door at one end and plenty of ventilation. It must be large enough that Puppy as an adult can stand up, turn around, and lie down comfortably in it. Bedding should be put into it for comfort. It is a boon to human and canine alike when properly used.

The crate becomes a dog's snug retreat. I prefer wooden crates, which Kent builds, because they're sturdy, make excellent "dens," and seem to be of a material with which puppies and dogs feel comfortable. Whatever kind of crate you choose, be sure that it has a door that can easily be

This is a fine crate for carrying a puppy, but not ideal for everyday use around the house because the door doesn't open fully.

left open. Crate-trained dogs like to go in and out of their crates at will, yet many of the plastic crates have inconvenient hanging doors that must be opened and closed by people. This feature makes the crate not a safe haven, but a cage. Unless the door is removed, such a crate doesn't work well.

Keep the crate at first in the room where people tend to congregate in your house. Soon after you've brought Puppy home, give him/her a toy or a treat in the crate. If need be, pick Puppy up and put her/him inside the crate. Leave the door open, and let Puppy snack or play inside the crate. Continue making the crate a place for treats for a few days, and as you place the treat and/or Puppy inside, say, "In your CRATE," emphasizing the last word. One day, casually close the crate door with Puppy inside, and go on about your business.

If you've done your initial training well, the crate is a good place where Puppy has been happy, and closing the door isn't going to result in puppy shrieks or tantrums. After a few minutes, open the crate door just as casually as you closed it, and let Puppy come out or stay inside as s/he chooses. If, however, Puppy throws a temper tantrum at the closed door, smack the side of the crate and say NO loudly. Do not let a tantrum win. Puppy does not come out of that crate until s/he has been quiet for at least a few minutes. When you do open the door, don't make a big deal of Puppy's freedom. This whole business of being or not being in the crate becomes a matter of course, not a test of wills. (Okay. So for a while, it may seem like a test of wills. Trust me—it gets better as you persevere.)

The earlier you teach Puppy to be in the crate, the easier. I went on a show trip with several Danes, including Burleigh, a friend's six-month-old Dane who hadn't been crate-trained. Putting Burleigh in his crate the first couple of days was like putting socks on an octopus. His owner and I each had to put each one of Burleigh's legs into the crate, several times per leg, repeating "Crate!" all the while. But in three days, Burleigh responded to the "Crate!" command as readily as the rest of the Danes who knew what they were doing, and the training lasted him the rest of his life.

Once your puppy knows the "Crate!" command, you can send it to that safe place whenever you want it out from underfoot or want to know it's up to no mischief. Closed in its crate, Puppy is safe and so is the rest of the house while you run some errands or go to a movie. During the night, a puppy sleeping in its crate isn't piddling on the rugs or teething on the cat. Soon you'll wonder how you lived without a crate.

But be very clear: The crate is haven and safety, not a substitute for proper training. It is neither punishment nor prison. No puppy or dog should have to spend hours and hours crated because its people don't want it around. The crate is not a replacement for a pen when you have to leave Puppy while you go to work. What you're working toward with crate training is having a place where your puppy can always go, be it to think, nap, gnaw on a toy, or get away from guests who stay too long.

Outside Quarters

Unless yours is a city/apartment dog, you'll probably want to provide outside quarters. Even in remote country areas, letting a puppy run loose is unwise at best. Basically, Puppy, allowed to run loose, comes to view you as a robot that puts out food and water—period. Bonding doesn't take place, you abdicate your alpha status, and you have a wild dog on your hands. If your dog isn't hit by a car or mauled by a larger dog, it's shot by a neighbor who thinks it's running sheep or cattle, or turned into a pound by someone who picks it up. As our world becomes more crowded, dogs are less and less safe running loose in it.

I consider a secure pen with attached sleeping quarters ideal as outside quarters for a dog. Why not a totally fenced yard? Well, not only can that be expensive, but also you and your dog may have differing opinions about landscaping. Providing a pen that your dog can dig in to its heart's content, bury puppy biscuits in, and loll in comfort is beneficial to you both. I've had dozens of woeful calls about ragged roses, uprooted shrubs, and destroyed flower beds, all casualties of young dogs taking over yards. Later, in Chapter 6, I'll deal with strategies to teach a dog to respect your part of the yard, because we all want to enjoy our dog's companionship as much as possible.

Just as crates shouldn't be prisons, neither should pens be cages. You'll need sturdy wire. Chain link is ideal but not the only choice; however, chicken wire is too flimsy to do the job. Even if you have a meek little dog, some wandering hulk of a dog might crash through a chicken wire fence and hassle your dog. The pen ought to be at least 4 feet (1.3 m) high, and 6 feet (2 m) would be better. Again, think about not only who might jump out, but also who might jump in. If you have a digger, set the fence in cement footings. It's eminently satisfying to watch a world-class digger not be able to burrow out of a pen! For large dogs, 10 feet (3.3 m) is a minimum width for a pen. Narrower than that and you'll have a dog with a bloody tail

from wagging it against the fence. If your dog is to spend the daytime in its pen when you're away at work, consider 10 feet (3.3 m) x 15 feet (5 m) as a minimum size. Don't make the pen too large. We built one kennel with 20 feet (6.6 m) x 40 feet (13 m) pens, which were a disaster for keeping our dogs in show condition! Our dogs romped and ran and insulted each other through their fences, and we never could keep any weight on them. Obviously, you'll scale the size down for smaller dogs, but make the pen generous. Sand or pea gravel are good for pen surfaces; both wear nails down, but neither is hard on feet and legs. Resist cement flooring pens; they're sheer hell on a dog's feet and legs. We rescued Thor, a young Dane who'd spent 45 days in a boarding kennel with cement pens and sleeping quarters. He was barely hobbling,

Your lively puppy should not be crated for hours on end.

and his feet were splayed flat—in less than two months! The house, grass, gravel pens, and plenty of calcium and vitamin C got Thor back, literally, on his feet.

Even if you decide to attach your dog's pen to a garage or other outbuilding, provide an insulated sleeping box accessible to the pen but separate from the rest of the outbuilding. Make sure the box is big enough for comfort—that is, for standing up, sprawling, and moving around. Danes and other large dogs need boxes 4 feet (1.3 m) x 4 feet (1.3 m) x 8 feet (2 m). Offset the entry so there's a nice, nestlike corner where your pup can get out of the wind. Straw makes excellent kennel bedding. It's springy, clean, and recyclable. I've made the mistake of putting old blankets in the kennels, and even dignified adult Danes have torn them to shreds and strewn the remains around the outside pens. There are two reasons to provide the sleeping box—comfort and safety. The 4 feet (1.3 m) height

means that Puppy needs to warm only that amount of room on a cold winter day. And whatever you are storing in the rest of the building isn't accessible to a curious, bored puppy. Outside quarters should be safe, comfortable, and clean. If you choose a commercially built dog house, make sure it has a floor raised off the ground, is well insulated, weatherproof, and roomy enough for your dog's comfort when it's adult. Avoid placing a doghouse near the fence in your pup's pen. Any half-smart puppy will jump onto the roof of the doghouse and from there over the fence.

Many people ask about chaining a dog. Consider this: A chained dog is vulnerable to everything that passes by. There is the chance of getting wrapped in the chain; many dogs have choked to death. The line run between two trees puts a puppy at risk of getting its line wrapped around a tree and choking. A valuable, purebred dog is easy to steal off a chain. And there's an ambiance of imprisonment for a dog who spends much of its life at the end of a chain.

Our dogs like their pens. With our group of dogs, we play a complicated game of switch-a-dog, with everyone having time in the house with us on a rotating basis. When it's time to go back to the pen, it's not a struggle. In the pens, they can dig, insult dogs down the way in another pen, bark at birds, and keep their own hours. They know which pen is theirs and bound in readily.

The pen, like the outdoor house, should be generous in size.

Escape Artists

Pulling into the driveway one afternoon, Kent and I caught sight of what looked like a blue tidal wave with wagging tails going up the hill. Peering closely, we recognized the F-Troop, our current litter of puppies, loose upon the world. We called them enthusiastically, and they came wagging to us, pouring into the house in a tangle of legs and bodies, just delighted to see us. After we'd greeted them suitably and told them what splendid puppies they were, Kent went to reconnoiter, while I checked our answering machine for messages.

Later Kent and I had a good laugh, for between the answering machine and a perusal of the various barns, we knew exactly where those puppies had gotten out and where they'd been for several hours. They'd had a wonderful day, tearing up empty feed sacks in the sheep barn, tossing straw around in the lower barn, and visiting a couple of the close neighbors. The phone messages went along the lines of, "Maybe we're seeing Dane puppies, I don't know, but a bunch of them just ran past. We know you don't let them run."

But everybody who has dogs occasionally has an escape artist. One thing we learned early on: Always welcome the escape artist as you would your favorite prodigal. Always call your puppy cheerfully by name and bring it into the house for a visit, praise, and love. Thus Puppy learns that there's one fine place to

head for should someone leave a pen door unlatched. Rather than cruising the neighborhood, your pup comes right to its own door. Welcoming the wanderer pays off generously over the years, because your dog does not run "away"; it runs "to." Remember this principle and you'll save yourself a lot of grief. No dog with half a brain is going to volunteer at a door where s/he's going to be scolded!

Fun

Toys

Before you buy any toy for your puppy, ask yourself three questions: Is it breakable? If so, is whatever it's made of fully digestible? Will pieces of it get tangled in Puppy's throat or intestines? I know that getting positive answers of all those three is tough; our dogs ought to have full-time jobs as toy testers! But oh, how awful are the stories vets can tell

Puppies are the perfect recipe for fun, so invest in some safe toys.

43

about puppies dead from toys that were unsafe.

We all think first of a ball for a puppy. There's one kind of ball that stands up even to Danes. It's made of solid English rubber. Maybe over the years a few nicks get gnawed out of it, but that's the extent of the damage. I've found a jingle ball also of English rubber, and, unlike other jingle balls where soon it's the puppy that's jingling and not the ball, this one is intact after ten years. All others have been trashed in an afternoon. If you can't see a mark that tells you the toy is English rubber, smell the toy. If it smells like vanilla, it's probably the right kind. There are also sturdy tugs or pull-toys of English rubber.

Of all the cute little squeak toys, absolutely none has yet stood the Dane puppy test. However, there is one cute spiky hedgehog toy that lasts longer than others. Barbarella used to adore her green hedgehog, and we got a kick out of seeing her walking around with a row of green spikes rimming her mouth. But that was a toy that dogs could play with

only under supervision, for we knew it was destructible. I simply take a toy away from a puppy if the pup is intent only on destroying it, giving it instead something indestructible.

Chief in this category are chew bones made of nylon. None of our dogs is crazy about them; however, when they're new and still smell of whatever they're impregnated with, puppies will gnaw at them. There are also some big, fluffy hanks of fiber many vets sell as tugs, and lots of dogs just love these. Pet stores are selling hoof parings from cattle and smoked pigs' ears, and although I find them disgusting to look at, dogs like them and they're safe.

Once I thought rawhide bones were very safe toys. Kent and I used to take bets on how long a new rawhide would last, or which dog could demolish one the fastest. If you're certain that you have a dog that absolutely cannot demolish a rawhide bone, and if you're willing to monitor the puppy's play, taking the rawhide away if the pup begins to chew off pieces and swallow them, probably rawhide bones are okay. However, I've learned from vets that the slimy strips of chewed rawhide can choke a dog by getting tangled around its esophagus, or the strips can cause intestinal obstruction, so we're not buying rawhide now.

It's vital that your puppy have something of its own to chew on. Between three and five months, when a puppy's teething, it's going to gnaw. If you don't provide legal gnawing matter, Puppy's going to demolish something illegal—maybe your best shoes, or the footstool by the couch. Just as you would with a toddler, take the illegal stuff away from Puppy and substitute its own toy. Though there are many voices raised against them, raw beef knucklebones are one of my top choices to give a teething puppy. The adult dogs can destroy a knucklebone, but a pup can't and that bone will give it many hours of comforting gnawing.

Make absolutely clear distinctions between what's yours and what's Puppy's while Puppy is young. Older, trained dogs can handle nuances; pups can't. Thus if you give Puppy an old running shoe that's run its last to chew on, you have no one but yourself to blame when Puppy disembowels one of your new Crosstrainers! Once a pup knows the difference between "yours" and "mine," you can blur the lines. We tie knots in Kent's worn-out work socks, and our dogs love to play tug-of-war with them.

Recent surveys have discovered that many dogs prefer soft toys to chewy ones. Watching seven-month-old Cordy grab soft things like sweaters and wool socks and run off to his bed with them, I wondered what he'd do with his very own teddy bear. Friends gave me a very worn teddy bear for Cordy, and he treasured it. Yes, he ripped it up, and yes, I took out the bear's eyes before Cordy could swallow them. But the teddy bear was his number one favorite toy, one he took great

comfort from. It got very ratty-looking, and I mended it a lot before I found the Mother Lode of inexpensive stuffed toys to replace it with.

You'll find all kinds of soft toys at pet supply stores. Some of the toys are relatively indestructible (speaking in Great Dane terms, that is!). Some are pretty pricey. I have discovered that second-hand stores like the Salvation Army or St. Vincent De Paul stores usually have a fine selection of used stuffed toys at wonderfully reasonable prices. Remove all trimmings that could cause gastric problems

It's vital that you give Puppy something safe to chew on.

Almost anything that's left lying around can become a toy. Just make sure that the object is safe for Puppy and of no special value to you.

before you give the stuffed toy to your pup, and replace the toy with a newer one when it becomes nothing but stuffing leaking all over the house.

By the way, even older dogs seem to take comfort from stuffed toys. Cordy still occasionally takes his teddy bear to bed with him at night, and he always finds it to carry around when he comes in from his pen.

Play Nicely!

A word of caution about play: Do not encourage Puppy to growl at you, even in play. Yes, this behavior is sort of cute in a funny little puppy that trips over its own feet. How cute would the same behavior be in, say, a full grown Akita? At the first sign of play growling, swat the puppy under the muzzle, say NO sharply, and go on with the game. If growling continues, make your swats sharper. Do not let this deteriorate into a contest of wills. Growling is dominant behavior. You, not Puppy, are to be the dominant one. If you start losing your temper, discontinue the game and try another day. But keep at it until Puppy knows that growling is not acceptable.

Nor should you allow Puppy to play with or bite at human hands. Right from the start, a pup must learn not to take the human hand in its mouth except seriously. If you teach the first lesson correctly, the second one comes naturally. One remedy for biting the hand in play is to grab the pup's lower jaw in your closed hand, give it a little shake, and say sharply, NO! Considering the dominance aspect, you, not the puppy, now control its biting apparatus. Be watchful, though, that no one else is playing with the puppy's mouth and encouraging unacceptable behavior.

There's a comb and a brush that's just right for your pup's coat length and density.

Grooming

We'll deal with grooming in Chapter 7, but as long as the Procurement Department for Canine Essentials is open, let's look at the basics.

Unless you've bought a smooth dog, get a brush now. You either brush the hair off the dog or you vacuum it off the carpet, so the sooner Puppy learns to love to be brushed, the less work you have to do. Confer with the shop owner about the best brush for your breed of puppy.

A basket of Boston terrier pups—once one of America's favorite dogs.

For a tiny puppy, toenail clippers like the ones you use yourself will do. If you're dealing with a giant, you're going to need heavy-duty canine nail clippers. Don't be an easy mark for a lot of fancy stuff—just a good pair of clippers. And some cauterizing powder, in case you hit the quick.

You'll likely already have bought Puppy's toothbrush and toothpaste from your vet. If you haven't, look for a canine toothbrush that fits over one of your fingers; they're easy to use. Get canine toothpaste. The human products will not do.

Other than these items, grooming niceties you may want to work up to can wait. But the earlier you teach Puppy about coat, nails, and teeth, the easier the lessons are.

Chapter 4
Out and About with Your Puppy

Now that you've completed the initial trip to your vet and the canine monster is somewhat protected from virulent diseases, it's time to get out and about. It's vital that Puppy know from the start that people are wonderful inventions who mean nothing but good times, pats, and maybe hugs. One of the most lasting mistakes people can make with young pups is to keep them so isolated that they don't learn to love all kinds of people. Now is the time to help your puppy to become sociable with people.

Puppy will learn to come more quickly if you get down to its level.

Early Leash Training

In order to make the best first impression with your puppy, you need to do some initial leash training. This might be a safety precaution, too; with Puppy firmly on leash, you're not running the risk of having him/her dashing heedlessly into traffic when you do go visiting.

Find a quiet, safe place to practice your first leash lessons. Put the leash on Puppy and go to the end of the leash. Squat down facing your puppy, call it by name, jerk the leash slightly, and say, "Come!" As the puppy starts toward you, hop/duck walk backwards, continuing to tell your puppy to come. Intersperse lots of praise among the "Come!" commands. Repeat this exercise for five minutes or so—or until you need a break from what is admittedly an awkward position. During this lesson, lavish praise for any of Puppy's efforts toward compliance are vital. This whole business, you want to emphasize right from the start, is wonderful fun. For now you are not concerned with how straight Puppy tracks, whether she ends up sitting on your left side in perfect obedience stance, or any other niceties except that Puppy associates your call, the leash tug, and the word "Come" with forward progress toward you.

But why, you may be thinking, must I assume such a cramped, uncomfortable position? I developed this method of leash training from an episode in Konrad Lorenz's book *King Solomon's Ring,* where he tells about impressing goslings. When he mentioned that he had to get down low enough to the ground that his voice would come from approximately the same height as a mother goose's voice in order for the goslings to "believe" the voice and hence impress, a light went on in my mind. Why do very small puppies often become hysterical during their first few leash lessons? Simple: They cannot see any part of their owner except shoes and knees. They're tied up in a strange line, being pulled they know not where or why, and a faraway voice way up high is telling them something strange.

But if they can see their owner, if the voice comes nearly from their own level, and if the reason for obeying an alien command is always visible, they stay calmer and progress in their lesson faster. As soon as I put this method of early leash training into practice, I had faster and better results. I think you'll be pleasantly surprised at how fast Puppy catches on to coming on

leash when called and at how little hysteria you'll have to cope with.

The reason I suggest a quiet, safe, *private* place for this exercise is that you might cause some hysterical laughter among the neighbors should they be watching your antics!

Once you've gotten Puppy coming enthusiastically while on leash, begin some informal heeling exercises. With Puppy on your left side, step out briskly, starting off with your left foot (so Puppy learns to associate the

Top: Select a quiet, safe, private place for training Puppy.

Bottom: Be lavish in your praise when Puppy responds to your call.

movement of your left leg with the start of a walk). Give the leash a little tug and say cheerfully, "Come, Puppy!" Keep up a cheerful patter while you're walking along. Throw in lots of "Oh, what a good Puppy!" as you cheer your pup along. I found Barbara Woodhouse's "*What* a good dog!" expression really seems to

cheer a dog up. The more fun early training is, the more your puppy will look forward to it and cooperate.

And what if Puppy sits down and won't come along?

Go back to the pup, squat down, pet it, cheer it up, do the hop/come routine again, praise, and move right into the walking along business. NEVER drag your puppy. All you're teaching is that you're bigger and stronger than the pup, and we knew that already.

Even if you get only a few feet of Puppy's walking along with you, praise and pet. Everybody starts somewhere.

One final note here—always quit while you're ahead! If you feel yourself getting frustrated, go back to an exercise Puppy knows, do it, praise, and quit for the time being. You're planning on a long life together with your pup; you don't have to teach everything today.

Watchdogs and Guard Dogs

Many people begin with the idea that they are going to turn their armful of giggly puppy into a fierce macho dog. To do that, they intend to keep their puppy away from everyone except the family. This is the wrong approach. Folks who train guard and attack dogs professionally will tell you that the only dogs suitable for such training are dogs who basically dote on people.

Friendly, goofy Killer, whom I always think of as a marshmallow, was what trainer friends considered a prime attack dog candidate because of his lovely temperament. Neither timid nor overly aggressive, Killer became my big, strong, brave guardian whenever he and I were out alone in strange or dark places. Kent, whom Killer preferred to me, he didn't especially protect, apparently convinced that Kent could take care of himself. We had put Killer into the show ring when he was six months old, let other people handle him in the ring, and he learned early to trust people.

The single best thing to do to bring up a dog that's going to be your protector is to take the puppy into your home, love her or him, introduce the pup to all your friends, family, and neighbors, and create a strong bond of love and trust between puppy and people. When your puppy matures, you'll be rewarded with absolute loyalty and protection. You'll have a dog that's far better than the iffy attack dogs— you'll have a natural defender. Bob and Carol took home Caliban, their black Dane, when he was eight weeks old. When Cal was nearly a year old, Carol and Bob had their second child. From the day they brought the baby home from the hospital, Carol told me, Cal decided no one was walking through their door without either Bob or Carol inviting them in. This wasn't behavior either adult had taught their big puppy; in true working dog fashion,

he figured that times had changed with a new baby in the house, protection was the order of the day, and that was his job. He was equally conscientious about the older child as she began to toddle around outside the house. With no discernible training, Caliban decided what the boundaries of their yard were, and when the toddler exceeded those bounds, he gently but firmly took hold of her clothes and brought her back where she belonged. Carol isn't the only Dane owner who remarked. "I didn't know I was getting a built-in babysitter when I got my puppy." However, in all cases where such a bond exists, the pup's early training has been love, being adopted into the heart of the family, and seeing lots of people.

Especially the working and herding breeds of dogs have an innate desire to keep their family safe. This inbred tendency will come to the fore naturally; all you have to do is provide love and get your puppy socialized

Even the distractions of traffic and unfamiliar surroundings do not phase these obedient youngsters.

early on. Take it wherever you can—safely, of course. Early leash training means you can go for walks in crowded places. Encourage strangers to pat and admire your puppy. Especially if you don't have children, recruit other people's children to play with your puppy. If you do have children, never mind that their version of leash training may not be as organized as yours; the bonding and fun that child and puppy are enjoying is vitally important. Do, however, be careful that you don't let a small child try to control a puppy that's too big in a situation where child and/or pup can get hurt.

No Fighting

The socializing that Puppy needs after leaving its mother and littermates is with people, not with other dogs particularly. At eight weeks old, a pup begins looking over the human crop, seeking its own person or people.

Insist that your puppy be gentle.

Canine socializing has been accomplished in the litter; for the next few months, get Puppy out with people.

At some point, though, you'll need to reintroduce Puppy to other dogs. If you have older dogs in the family, the older dogs have told Puppy who's the boss dog, and that matter is settled. Nonfamily dogs are another matter. Dogs always test dominance. It's their nature. The only dog tends to believe that next to its alpha human, it's the top dog in the world. This attitude is fine unless it results in a dog that picks fights with every other dog it meets. You don't need a fighter. You don't need the vet bills a fighter will amass, nor the grief and worry, nor the scarred dog, nor the likely lawsuits.

Ideally, dogs that are strangers should be introduced while each is under the owner's control, be it leash or voice control. Let them go nose to nose and sniff, but at the first sign of growling or hackling, give a loud, firm NO. If the behavior persists, separate them immediately. Growling from a distance is unacceptable, too. Correct this with a quick smack under your dog's muzzle, accompanied by another loud NO. Growly behavior on the part of a puppy to an adult dog isn't cute; it's dangerous and could get the young fool mauled. There are places—the vet's office is one—where you don't want your puppy either to challenge or romp up to other dogs. When you take Puppy through an obedience class, you'll get a lot of help in teaching her or him to ignore other dogs.

Yet you may have friends with dogs that you want to be able to visit and not have your respective dogs kill each other. There are still remote beaches where we can walk with our dogs, and none of us wants to cause dogfights in such places. Many people take several dogs hunting together; fights are not part of the sport. A dog that attacks another with no cause is a danger to everyone. You owe yourself and your puppy adequate training to avoid such a menacing personality. It's another instance when what might be tolerable in a puppy will be positively indefensible in an adult dog.

Should you have to break up a dogfight, don't be squeamish. If there are two people, each should grab a set of back legs and pull the dogs apart. If you're alone, cuff, kick, and use your biggest, most authoritative voice. Become the nastiest, most menacing alpha dog any pack ever knew! You may be saving your dog's life, or the life of some harebrained dog that suffers from an overachiever complex. You do run the risk of getting accidentally bitten, you and the owner of the other dog may end up yelling at each other, and the entire scenario is ugly. The alternative, however, is one I and many other dog owners find absolutely unacceptable—that of having our dogs maimed and mauled. Avoiding fights is best.

Keep your leash handy wherever you go, even at a remote beach. Unless you're positive that your dog is absolutely under your voice com-

Supervise initial encounters with other dogs. Insist on no fighting.

mand, put your dog on leash at the approach of a strange dog and keep it on leash until you're sure there's no chance of fighting. Looking at the world from a dog's point of view is one of the best ways to prevent situations from going bad. To your protective dog, any other canine rushing up to you is a threat; that's why many fights begin. Even a placid dog is likely to be watchful in strange places, so the more control you exert, the less reason your dog will have to feel threatened. If you ride a bicycle and take your dog along, keep it on leash. This precaution will stop your dog from rushing at dogs you may encounter on the way. It seems as if being on leash is face-saving for a dog: S/he might attack the uprushing alien dog, but being so firmly under your control, don't you see, attack is impossible. Thus the two of you can take nice, peaceful rides.

Exercise

Puppies are like other babies; they play for a while, then go find a cozy place to nap. This natural behavior should be encouraged, and puppies should not be forced to play when they're tired. Your pup will learn to go for pretty much whatever kind of walks you like to take, but let Puppy train up to long walks. How long did it take you to work up to a five-mile jaunt? If you ride a bicycle, your pup will eventually like accompanying you for a reasonable ride, but do remember that you're riding and Puppy's walking the whole way. Pay attention to Puppy's behavior. If s/he slows down, tries to stop and lie down, or is panting, it's time to take a long rest, then head home at a gentle pace.

Equally important, consider how carefully you choose your footwear for long walks. Puppy has bare feet on. Veterinarians are seeing lots of dogs these days with raw, even bleeding foot pads from being forced to walk too far on hot, abrasive roads and walkways. Be considerate. Wash your dog's feet if chemicals have been spread on the roads you've used—either salt in places where it snows, or weed killers.

If you walk in traffic, think about the noxious fumes every passing car is emitting. Puppy is right down there at tailpipe level, breathing in a heavier dose of those fumes than you're getting. The exercise may be good, but the pollutants are loading up your dog's system. Again, consideration is vital.

The rule of thumb for puppy exercise is this: Don't force it.

Dogs and Water

Melville said in *Moby Dick,* "Set any man walking, and his feet will carry him to water." Women, children, and dogs, too, seem to head for water when they go walking. How you introduce a puppy to water can make a future water lover or water hater.

Rivers, Lakes, and Streams

Puppies seem less afraid of fresh than salt water. A clean stream or river with gently sloping banks is the ideal place to introduce a pup to water. You can slosh around together, Puppy isn't over its head and hence isn't scared, and there's no problem (we hope!) with drinking the water. Nor is it harmful left on Puppy's coat, though a long-eared dog should have its ears dried after you're done playing around.

Adjust your pace to a puppy's needs.

Don't let your puppy get chilled. We tend to forget that the canine cooling and heating system is different from ours. What seems like a lovely day basking in the sun for a person can be sheer torture for a dog, who doesn't have sweat glands like ours. And the brisk autumn day at the river, when we are dressed in our down jackets and hiking boots, is cold going indeed for a weimaraner or a Dane with only a thin coat of hair.

To the Sea

Time a pup's first trip to the ocean so you hit a low or ebbing tide. Heavy, crashing surf scares puppies. They can cope with gentle, lapping waves. Don't force them to swim. Let a puppy paddle along the shore and get comfortable with this new environment. Bit by bit, as Puppy gets bigger, you can swim out and invite Puppy to join you. Some will. Some won't. The hunting and retrieving breeds, including poodles, will take to water more readily than, say, Danes. Starbuck, my weimaraner, wouldn't stay out of water with birds in it, no matter what the season. Neither would he go into water without birds in it, also no matter the season. Gay, one of the family's boxers, swam all year on the Connecticut coast unless forcibly restrained. When she got tired in the water, she would use me as her raft, clambering aboard most rudely.

The scared dog in water is a danger to itself and others. I most definitely do not hold to the theory of

"Throw the dog overboard and it'll learn to swim." No one bothers to collect statistics on drowned dogs, not to mention terrified dogs who detest water. They thrash, claw, and scar anyone who gets in the way of their blind rush for dry land. Especially at the ocean, let your pup find its own sea legs. Be encouraging, but don't force the issue.

One experience you're likely to go through on early trips to salt water is that your pup will drink the stuff. Discourage this behavior. A few laps won't harm and will often teach a puppy that seawater is nasty to drink. But big gulps of seawater will result in one nauseated dog. It won't take more than a couple such bad experiences before your pup quits drinking seawater, but in the meantime, unless you forcefully intervene, plan on staying at the beach longer than you wanted to while Puppy barfs. If you bring a container of fresh water from home for your canine companion and you tell

Once Puppy has learned to like the water, you can have buckets of fun together.

Puppy "NO!" when it tries to drink the salt water, you'll be starting right on outings to the beach. That's part of being considerate.

Salt water is also harmful to a dog's coat. It's very drying. So after a trip to the sea, make sure your dog is well washed with fresh water. If you're dealing with a puppy, don't let the pup get chilled. Puppies take a relatively long time to maintain their normal body temperature, and early chills result in lots of sick puppies. Likewise, don't subject any dog to hours of baking in hot sun. Dogs do not perspire as we do, nor do they covet a golden tan. Instead, they burn and suffer in the hot sun.

The ancient Greeks had the right attitude toward all such trips to the water, exercise, walks, and so on: Everything in moderation. A well-exercised adult dog will be in good flesh and have solid, firm muscles. Most dogs, given adequate room and weekend outings with their people, will keep themselves in good shape. In my years of showing dogs, I've heard all sorts of stories about what one could do to get a dog "in show condition." These included such cruelties as running a puppy on leash behind a station wagon, supposedly to build muscles, and such bizarre aberrations as giving a dog a can of beer with his supper every night to put weight on him. Experience has taught me that each puppy matures at an individual speed; trying to change that biological clock is relatively useless.

Manners in the Car

In my lifetime I've had one dog so far who went through a period of being a jumpy rider. Blitz, my first weimaraner, paced, jumped from the back to the front seat, panted, and generally drove me crazy for several months of his young adulthood. Thinking like a dog, I realized that he was reacting to my own tension in heavy traffic. Attuned as he was to me, if I was tense, there must be something wrong with the situation. Since it was impractical for me to take tranquilizers in such a situation, I asked my vet about tranquilizers for Blitz. With the dog calmed down, I learned to calm down, too. Soon neither of us needed chemical intervention to enjoy time together in the car. Unfortunately, anything that causes you distress in a car is going to be transmitted to your puppy, and you'll be faced with a problem rider. If your pup comes up with strange behavior for which you can find no reason, check to see what danger signals you're sending—then see what you can do about how you feel! Perhaps there will be trips on which your dog won't accompany you, not for any dog reasons, but because you're having enough trouble coping with yourself and don't need to worry your dog.

First Trips

Most puppies are carsick to some extent. I've never seen one not get over car sickness, so don't despair. Don't feed a pup before a ride. Be sure your pup has "gone potty" before setting out. Make the first car trips short if you can. Carry paper towels and plastic bags for cleanup. Avoid bumpy, curvy roads if possible, and drive steadily. Preferably have someone with you to ride cleanup. For some reason, plain vanilla ice cream calms a puppy's stomach. Maybe a half-scoop of ice cream immediately before setting out is a good idea. Years ago, my family and I took eight boxer pups on a long trip to get their ears cropped. They were miserably, slimily carsick the entire journey to the vet's. He remarked as we were loading up for the trip home that vanilla ice cream was a cure for the carsickies. Those eight little boxers slurped their ice cream, eyes half-closed in puppy bliss. Then they piled up on each other and slept the rest of the way home.

Decide where you want your puppy to ride, then insist that it stay there. Here's where crate training comes in very handy! If your car's too small for a crate, simply put the puppy back where it belongs one more time than it hops over to where it doesn't belong! If I'm alone with a puppy that's going to get very big, I ride the pup next to me in the front seat on first trips. I can pet it and reassure it cheerfully about the joys of the open road. I can also tell what it's doing and plan ahead for a quick barf stop if need be. I know that eventually it'll outgrow the front seat and prefer the space in the back of a van or station wagon.

One strategy for dealing with exuberant canine passengers is to leash them and attach the leashes to a fixed object in the car. Years ago I lived with Ralph and George, the beagle brothers, the most obstreperous dogs I've ever known. I had a tiny red Fiat convertible, out of which Ralph and George leaped regularly whenever they saw anything interesting at a stoplight. It was dangerous, maddening, and not to be tolerated. I had two ring bolts welded onto the back wheelwells of the Fiat, one on each side. I got short traffic leashes with snaps on each end. From then on, the beagle brothers could stand up and look out of the open-topped convertible, but their leaping days were done. I did the same with a station wagon later, having liked the convenience of so easily restraining dogs where I wanted them in a car. There are also wire barriers that keep dogs from coming into the front of a car. And, finally, you might wish to check out the dog safety belts that are now available.

Crates make life easier in the car, too.

There are many ways of making life with puppies and dogs smooth!

Not Loose in Pickups

In California today it's illegal for an unrestrained dog to ride in the bed of a pickup truck. This wasn't a whimsical law; before the law was finally passed, countless dogs jumped or fell out of pickups, were injured, killed, or caused accidents. Much preferable to cross-tying a dog in a pickup bed are the canopies so readily available. Dogs don't get debris in their eyes and ears, are sheltered from sun or rain, and are safe. One couple referred to their pickup with canopy as "the fastest doghouse in the West." That's a fine compromise if you're carrying a big dog or several dogs. Be sure, though, that the truck bed has a liner to give your puppy good traction underfoot. It is miserable to slip and slide on a slick metal floor at 55 miles an hour!

No Wind in the Ears

Sometimes we see dogs riding with their heads out of car windows, their ears flapping in the breeze. The wind isn't good for dogs' ears—or their eyes, either. Open windows enough for noses to sniff the delicious scents of unfamiliar territory, but not enough for heads to hang out. Especially with electric windows, there's also the danger of someone hitting the wrong button and garroting the puppy. If the pup's head is hanging out of the rear window of a station wagon, your pup is inhaling exhaust fumes with every breath.

Dangers of Heat

Cars are the best rolling solar collectors there are! When these efficient heat collectors are parked, they're deadly to canines left inside them. Leaving a couple of windows open a crack absolutely does not provide enough air circulation for a trapped puppy during hot weather. Many cities have ordinances that allow rescue personnel to break into parked cars to free dogs left in circumstances that are potentially lethal. During hot weather, puppies or dogs should be left at home. Heat prostration happens fast and is often fatal. Especially young and especially old dogs are particularly vulnerable to ill effects from heat. Even an air-conditioned vehicle can get too hot for dogs. Some years ago Kent and I went on a show trip to Washington State during late June, taking with us two young Danes and DJ, who was nine years old. The temperature rose, and I turned the air conditioning on full blast. However, DJ was panting excessively and whining in his crate. Knowing that excessive panting is an early sign of heat prostration, I immediately went looking for other signs. Checking under his armpits, I found his temperature alarmingly high. With the panting, this told me that he wasn't handling the heat and was in danger, so I got him out loose in the van, directly under the air conditioner. As Kent sped toward the shady campground where we were going to spend the night, I slopped big towels in water and draped them over DJ, bringing his temperature down, which must be done to prevent heat prostration. The heat from the road beneath us scorched the floor of the van, and I made a thick padding of our sleeping bags to give old DJ more relief. The two younger dogs in their crates, which were raised off the van floor, were uncomfortable, but not in distress. That trip taught me that old show dogs stay home except during dependably moderate weather. The lesson ought to be applied to summer vacations in general; a good kennel is a better place for a dog than the unexpected vagaries of the road. A dog can go into heat prostration fast, and you can't always be sure of finding a cool place in strange locales.

If you positively must take your puppy or dog on a long car trip in hot weather, take plenty of water, make sure your dog isn't lying on a hot car floor, and have big towels handy to keep your dog wet. If your dog is

coated, carry some sort of spritzer so you can keep your pooch damp and cool during the trip. Above all, don't leave your dog in the car while you flounce off into an air-conditioned restaurant for a nice meal.

Even around town for short summer errands, if Puppy is going along, make your trips early in the morning before the heat is up. Many of the emergencies that end up at the vet's would never occur with foresight and thoughtfulness toward our canine companions.

A five-week-old German shepherd puppy resting after a midsummer romp.

Chapter 5
Early Lessons

There are three very good reasons for me not to include specifics on actual obedience training in this book, even though I not only consider such training vital but also run obedience classes myself. First, there are already excellent books available on the subject. (See Bibliography, page 106.) But the second reason is more important: The volume of my telephone calls over the years indicates that most problems people have with puppies are *not* the kinds of things covered in a standard obedience class. It's what I term the Life Problems that drive people crazy trying to civilize that hellion—the new puppy. Third, a book is a very poor

substitute for physically attending an obedience class. The combination of strange dogs, strange people, and a new place work together to speed your puppy's learning process. Therefore, I'll deal with those programs, tricks, dodges, and scams that Kent and I have used over the years in coping with the varieties of mischief that new puppies can cook up to amuse themselves and totally wreck a house—as well as the human minds around them. But before we charge into lessons and remedies, I urge you to get yourself and your puppy to an obedience class before the pup is six months old. The actual physical presence of other dogs, people, and the trainer combine into an experience that can't be duplicated, no matter how talented you may be in training a puppy. You'll be doing both of you a favor you won't regret.

Axiom One

Let us always keep Axiom One firmly in mind: *This New Puppy Is Not Any Other Dog You've Ever Owned.* No matter if s/he is the same breed as Dear Departed Bozo, with the same markings, bred out of the same line, fed the same diet, and even sleeping in the same bed, the new puppy is a distinct individual. True, there are and will be various breed characteristics that will be apparent. That's probably the best reason for getting a pup of a certain breed from an ethical breeder who understands and carefully follows the breed standard. But the standard implies a spectrum of possible behaviors. The new puppy may well be at another point on the allowable spectrum than the Dear Departed.

Also, D.D. was an old dog, used to your crotchets and special needs, grooved into your lifestyle. Puppy is a puppy, so don't be making those disparaging comparisons; chances are that you have wiped from your mind the hideous things D.D. did as a puppy! Now you're starting with a clean slate.

So, with all that in mind, let's get on with the program.

Consistency

A dog or a puppy absolutely thrives on consistency. This is true all the way from finding and sticking to the right kibble to deciding what is and what isn't acceptable behavior. Consistency makes a pup very, very much happier and more secure than the bouncy kind of life many of us humans prefer.

Maybe you'll have to have periodic family councils to hammer out just what kinds of canine behavior

are and are not acceptable to various members of the clan. By all means get it straight among the human members of the family; otherwise, if you're unpredictable and all pulling in different directions, Puppy will end up a confused mess. And it'll be your fault. Once you've agreed on what goes, enforce the rules. "Oh, let her do it just this once," is a sure way to wreck the training program and confuse the pup.

No two are ever really alike.

The Rule of Threes

People who raised Danes long before we got into the act gave us some good advice that works with all breeds. They said, "Anything you do three times with a Dane becomes tradition." Let me add to that the Rule of Three given me by my first obedience trainer: In teaching a new thing like "Heel," work your pup in three different places. Then the behavior becomes fixed in the pup's mind as something that must be done always and everywhere, not just at home or in the training hall. I have obedience students wail to me, "But he does it so perfectly at home!" when their pup is goofing off by the numbers during class. Right away I recognize someone who trains only in the peaceful confines of the backyard.

So. Work in threes. Don't worry about whether three is a mystical number having some deep occult significance for dogs. Be a pragmatist and take my word for it: Three items or three places is a charm!

Thus the three times you're too lazy to correct some bad habit also become a charm—for the puppy, that is, who sees correction isn't forthcoming and hence believes the behavior must be okay.

Consistent Vocabulary

Puppy probably comes to you having either no vocabulary or a very limited one. Decide your words of command and make the whole family use only those words. I despair when I observe people chattering away, nagging and nagging their puppies with the vocabulary of human adults, then wondering why the poor, silly puppies don't seem to get the message. Kent and I had a discussion some years back about the terms we used to encourage a puppy to eliminate outside. He was, I think understandably, somewhat put off at standing around telling a huge Dane puppy to "Go potty." I

find that term comfortable and easily understood by a pup. However, as I agreed with him then and still do, use any term that's easy to understand— which means short—and comfortable, as long as that's the terminology you always use for that particular behavior. With Star, whom we were housebreaking at the time, Kent got outstanding results by telling her first to "make a puddle," then telling her to "go poop." We won't get into semantic nitpicking over whether his terms are any more dignified than my all purpose "go potty"; with Star, Kent's terms work—always. And it was always Kent's terms that I used with Star. After all, those were the words she understood.

There's another all-purpose word I've used over the years with puppies: GENTLE. Drawn out and said slowly, the word sounds like the behavior I'm encouraging. When a puppy is playing too roughly, for instance, a calming hand accompanied by the repetition of the "Gentle" command will serve to quiet the situation. The puppy isn't doing something essentially wrong when you want the "Gentle" command—it's just doing too much or too vigorously. So, the curious puppy that is nosing a resident cat will be warned to be GENTLE. I want the puppy and the cat to get along—insist on it, in fact—so this is not a time for NO. Obviously the older dog that knows "Gentle" will understand what it's doing wrong if it gets too rough with a puppy. The puppy who greets someone too rambunctiously is throttled down, as it were, with the "Gentle!" warning. If you think of the "NO" as a red light, "Gentle" is the amber, or warning, light. A very useful command, I've found.

Not Chewing on People

One of a puppy's habits that gets old fast is that of biting or chewing on your hands, arms, ankles—whatever protrudes. If your puppy is still doing this at eight weeks or older, chances are that someone (maybe even you) once thought it was cute. Now it hurts. Later it will become downright dangerous.

Now is the time to correct the bad habit. Never—not even once again—let Puppy bite/chew on you. At the first nibble, shout "NO!" and swat Puppy with your fingers lightly under the jaws. Be sure it's under. Remember, dogs don't connect the swat under the jaws with a human hand and hence don't become hand-shy.

"But won't I run the risk of making my pup bite its tongue?" I am asked when I share this corrective method.

The answer is, "Probably not." Surely you're not going to make the initial swats so power-packed that you knock your pup's teeth out. You are capable of discretion.

For young pups still in the whelping box, I use very light taps. Seldom do I have to get rougher because from the start I discourage

This kind of play defeats your training program.

the chewing and biting that I, along with many others, find obnoxious. Agreed, I'm lucky since Kent and I get to start most of our puppies and thus have the advantage of not having to cope with ingrained bad habits. However, we did buy Starshine from a Midwestern breeder who didn't follow our methods, and Star came out of her flight crate nipping and joyously teething on every limb she could reach, so we had to change already developed behavior. I know it takes longer than starting out right! With Star, who was definitely stubborn, the process of discouraging her nipping took months and many swats under the muzzle, hindered by the fact that Kent thought she was the cutest thing that had ever torn through a house. The swats had to get very sharp and the "NOs!" very loud. Interestingly, Star quit teething on me long before she gave up on Kent. Like all bright puppies, she knew what she should get away with and on whom.

If the biting goes on and isn't corrected by the smacks under the jaw, try taking the puppy's lower jaw in your hand and giving the jaw a slight shake as you say "NO!" Your hand in the puppy's mouth and your interruption of its ability to bite is very dominant behavior. You're controlling its biting process—you must be the boss!

Not Jumping up on People

It's important to learn the difference between "OFF!" and "DOWN!" When you get into obedience work, you'll use the command "DOWN!" to mean that the pup will lie down. Therefore, while you're working on the problem of jumping up on or at you, don't use the wrong command. Tell Puppy "OFF!"

And what if s/he doesn't? Let's examine why a puppy jumps before we try to eradicate jumping. Have you ever greeted someone you love and been able to see only that person's ankles? Don't you want to look into the face of your beloved? So does your puppy, so, being very short, it jumps up to see you. The first thing you can do to begin to eradicate the unacceptable jumping is bending or squatting down to greet your puppy. You bend and Puppy doesn't have to jump up to see your face. That's an important beginning.

Second, every time Puppy jumps up on you, take his/her front paws,

put Puppy off you firmly, and while you're doing this, say "OFF!" loudly and firmly. If you do this, coupled with the bend-over greeting, while Puppy is still young, you have no need for rougher methods. Remember to pat Puppy and say "Good Puppy" as soon as all four feet are on the floor. Praise *must* always follow any attempt by the pup to do what you've demanded, even if the attempt is a pretty casual version of what you have in mind as ideal compliance. Your praise is Puppy's reward for good behavior.

Knee-Jerk Reaction

However, maybe you have, say, a year-old Airedale who has been running your life his way before you read this. You don't need me to tell you that you have a problem! You're going to have to get rougher than the behavior described above if you want results.

I suggest a knee-jerk reaction. When you see your dog coming at you to jump, bring your knee up fast against his chest. At the same time, shout "NO. OFF!" Do this every time. You may even shove with your knee. Knocking the dog down once or twice may be beneficial to it in getting the message across; certainly it'll be beneficial to you in working off some frustrations.

There are trainers who suggest stepping on the jumper's back toes. You may be faster and better coordinated than I am, so this method may work for you. It never has for me.

Down Immediately on Command

While we're on the subject of up or down, consider seriously one command you're going to teach Puppy in obedience class—the "DOWN" command. This single word may be the most important one s/he learns. Insist that Puppy go into a Down immediately on your voice command and stay there until released. Work on this exercise after you've leash-trained your puppy, as often you'll need the leash to get the puppy into a DOWN position. With the puppy in front of you, bend over and command "DOWN!" tugging the leash downward as you say the word. You may have to pull gently on the leash from the front and push gen-

tly on the puppy's rear, just above its hip bones. Once you get the puppy down, follow with the command "STAY!" Keep your pup in a down position for a minute, then release it with a cheerful "Okay!" If your puppy keeps getting up, put your foot on the leash and leave no slack in that leash, thus forcing the pup to remain down. Work up to several minutes by the time it's eight months old or so. Remember when the exercise is over to pet or praise your GOOD DOG. Keep working on "DOWN!" until you get instant compliance the first time you give the command. Consider: You're out walking and Puppy is off leash. You call Puppy to come to you, but while Puppy is approaching you, you see danger, perhaps a speeding car, between you and Puppy. Being able to interrupt Puppy's approach with a DOWN

Teaching your puppy the DOWN command can save its life.

65

These are the hand signals for the advanced DOWN command.

will save its life. Because this is such an important command, teach it in all its ramifications as soon as possible. There's the raised arm/dropped arm signal that means "DOWN" in advanced obedience work. I urge you to incorporate this signal in Puppy's training early, right after you've insured that Puppy drops on your verbal command. Thus, if there's a lot of noise and perhaps Puppy won't hear your spoken "DOWN," you can reinforce it with the arm signal, giving double assurance that Puppy's forward progress will be interrupted. Too often all of us are sloppy about the DOWN command, accepting slow or grudging response. Promise yourself that this time, with this puppy, you're going to provide yourself—and Puppy—with a strong tool for potential lifesaving.

Not Charging the Door

Another annoying habit of many dogs is that of charging the door when someone knocks. Since the dog is likely to run faster than the resident human, the dog thinks it's out of your range and hence only under voice control. Now having your dog thoroughly under voice control is a situation to be striven for, but it doesn't come overnight. In the meantime, how to cope? I first used one of those chain collars that's supposed to be keyed so it would assault the dog's ears when it was jangled, for I had an adult, incorrigible door charger, Heidi. One day when Heidi was charging the door, I couldn't immediately find the sound collar, so I just grabbed a regular chain choker and threw it, hitting the door at the same moment that my voice hit her ears with the NO. The effect was the same: She backed off. Thus I learned that one doesn't need any special equipment; the jangle of any choke chain suddenly landing out of thin air is upsetting enough to cause your dog to heed your NO command. Repeated regularly, this combination of the thrown chain and the NO command resulted in Heidi's not charging doors anymore—in fact, she charged them a lot less, and finally not at all. I've used the technique since on other dogs who learned the lesson in just two or three sessions.

Don't worry about what the person at the door is going to think when you go through your correctional antics. People don't think kind thoughts when they're knocked down or jumped on by a dog that answers the door, so they're likely to appreciate your efforts to keep their entry safe.

Besides using the thrown object indoors to aid training, thrown objects are useful outdoors, too. Put some pebbles into an empty plastic bottle and use it as an outdoor training aid. The puppy who doesn't heed your voice command is startled by the rattle the bottle makes landing nearby and is quickly convinced that it's not safe to ignore you. A clod of dirt or a handful of pebbles will do in a pinch. Don't use anything that would hurt your pup if it hit. The object here is to get Puppy's attention, not to touch her/him. The combination of the thrown object and your command

gets the pup's attention and improves compliance. Be sneaky about throwing things; you don't want Puppy to see you doing the throwing, for that could make the pup afraid of you.

Coming When Called

It's best if you don't take your puppy off leash outdoors until you're rock sure s/he is thoroughly dependable on such niceties as coming when you call, but we all sometimes make mistakes and overestimate how well trained a pup is. Having done just this, you call your puppy, who comes beautifully when on a training leash. Puppy doesn't come. Call again, timing your call so it hits Puppy's ears at the same second that the thrown object hits the ground right by Puppy's head. The shock of having an unknown and unexpected object strike next to it will cause the pup to consider that safety lies at your side, not out there where strange objects can come hurtling out of the air. It seems that the outrage of having an unexpected something land nearby is enough to cause a puppy to return to you, for you represent safety.

Walk Away

In this same department of not coming when called is that favorite game of prankster puppies, See How Fast Owner Can Run. Depend on it, this is a game you will never

Top: Chasing your puppy is a no-win game.

Bottom: Always reward your puppy for coming to you.

win! Oh, you'll get your exercise all right, but always at the last instant Puppy will scoot out from your grasp and frisk away, eager for the game to continue. The secret here is never to play the game. Instead, make sure Puppy sees you as you turn smartly and authoritatively away from the direction in which Puppy is frisking. Walk determinedly away from Puppy, telling it sharply "COME!" Let determination and purpose show in every nuance of your body language.

Puppy is now confused. You're not playing by its rules. Furthermore, and much worse, you seem to be actually leaving Puppy out in the world alone where who-knows-what might happen. After some uncertainty and a short time to test whether you really mean what you're doing, Puppy will follow you. When it gets to your side and you put the leash back on, pats and praises are in order, no matter how many palpitations your heart is having.

THE FIRST TIME THAT YOU SMACK YOUR DISOBEDIENT PUPPY WHEN IT COMES TO YOU IS THE LAST TIME YOUR PUPPY WILL COME TO YOU WILLINGLY.

This trick of walking away from the puppy that won't come is hard and demands all your self-discipline and willpower. It works, though, and it prevents the start of a no-win game. When there are loose dogs at dog shows, every owner gets ready to snag the running dog, for here we have a situation where the dog is lost, frightened, and likely to get into trouble. I've found that in most groups of people, someone is likely to detain the fleeing dog, so the risks aren't as great as they may seem.

To close this subject, some breeds are more adventurous than others and more prone to wandering. A hound on a trail just about can't hear its owner's call. I had friends whose basset hound would run right over their feet without knowing it when he was on a rabbit trail in the woods. Sighthounds such as Afghans and salukis seem to have their ears and brains disconnected from everything except the chase when they're on a trail, so you don't take such dogs out loose unless they're in a safe place. The sensible working and herding breeds—Danes, corgis, all the shepherds, Great Pyrenees, and such—don't want to be away from their people and often herd the people. However, an unhappy working or herding dog will often run away from a bad home in search of something better. That's how I got my most recent refugee from an animal shelter. She was picked up by Animal Control for wandering, and, only hours before she was due to be killed, I got word of her existence. I saved her life, brought her home, kept close watch on her trips outdoors for several weeks, and made her welcome. In more than two years, having found the place where she wants to be, she's never wandered.

Teaching Exterior Boundaries

While you're doing early training, restrain your puppy from leaving your yard except on leash and with a person. Any time Puppy steps outside the boundaries of your yard without you, give a sharp NO, bring the pup back inside the boundaries, and praise her/him for returning. Day by day, enforce that sense of territoriality. You're creating an invisible fence around your yard. Persistence in doing this will give you a dog who doesn't wander out of your yard. Passing joggers, children, bicyclists, and so forth are safe, and so is your dog. Admittedly some breeds of dogs are easier to teach this than others; the sporting breeds, for instance, are easily lured away. Once upon a time when we were thinly populated, one could live in the country and let a setter have a good day's roam with little danger, but those days are gone. The larger the dog, the more people in general fear it, and the more danger that dog is in if it's wandering loose. Further, people have become more prone to sue for any untoward event, real or imagined. In response to this, most localities have strict laws against free-ranging dogs. The amount of legal trouble a loose dog can cost any of us is not to be believed. In defense of your bank account, as well as of your dog's safety, teach Puppy that there's no place like home!

Invisible Fences

The "invisible" or electronic fence is an intriguing product of the electronic age. Basically, this fence is a buried wire connected to a transmitter. The wire can be placed around whatever perimeter of your yard you do not want your dog to cross. When your pet goes outside, it must wear a special collar that receives messages from the transmitter. When puppy gets into the no-go range, the collar signals. The closer to the buried wire the dog goes, the stronger (and more

A samoyed puppy at full trot.

annoying) the collar signal becomes. This mechanism functions the way electronic no-bark collars work. Now, although the collar is tuned to a specific signal, there's no guarantee that that signal won't be over-ridden by a more powerful signal even as much as five miles away.

It's entirely possible that in a few sessions, your dog may become dependably trained to respect the invisible barrier and thus be able to go outside without the electronic collar on. So if you live in a place where you aren't allowed to put up a visible fence, the electronic fence is a possible answer to a training problem.

I find one further problem with this kind of fence: While it may teach your dog to stay *in* your yard, it does nothing to keep wandering dogs *out*.

In the final analysis, the old-fashioned method of actually getting your dog to know where the boundaries are and to respect them has a longer-lasting benefit than paying big money for a short-cut. Many of us move from place to place. When our dogs know what we mean by respecting boundaries, it's easy to teach them where the perimeters are in the new place. If they know only the discomfort of an electronic reminder, then we're stuck with buying a new invisible fence every time we move.

A final word on fences, boundaries, and training. If you don't have the time, patience, and/or consistency to teach your dog what the boundaries are, then put up a fence, or fence part of the yard. You're not being a failure as a dog owner; you're being honest and realistic. What can happen to your dog outside its own yard includes being hit by a car, poisoned, attacked by other dogs, turned into the animal control authorities, stolen—think of something dire, and some dog has experienced it. And even if you think your dog is dependable, as one Connecticut veterinarian put it about dogs wandering or not wandering, "they can all be bought." The fragrance of a female in heat three miles away is a far more powerful motivator to a dog than your possible displeasure! And a sturdy, non-climbable fence is a powerful deterrent to the dog with the urge to wander.

The Old Mousetrap Trick

One of the secrets of puppy and dog training is finding strategies that work when Puppy thinks either you're not within reach or not even present. Lessons obeyed only under your immediate control are very shaky. What you're after is lessons that will stick whether you're on the scene or not. These often take some ingenuity on your part.

It was that goofy marshmallow, Killer, who pushed me into trying one of the Mousetrap Tricks. In dog training, Mousetrapping is one of those genius corrections that work when you're not immediately present. It works even if you're not at home. Simply, buy several little mousetraps—the old-fashioned kind that has a hinged wire trapfall that goes "Snap!" when the spring that holds it in readiness is released. For your purposes you'll not need any bait. What you want from the mousetrap is its noise and its surprise value. Here's one of the ways Mousetrapping worked for me. Killer had a passion for my indoor potted plants; I was living with a pathetic, ragged array of greenery. The thing of it was, I could never catch him eating plants, and when I accused him of it, he went cross-eyed and pleaded complete mental incompetence.

So I ringed the largest plant— what was left of a lovely gardenia— with four mousetraps, set and almost hidden by the remaining greenery. To my absolute delight, I was in the next room when I heard the first mousetrap snap. I tiptoed to the door in time to watch Killer root curiously in the plant pot, setting off another mousetrap. He leaped back-ward, totally amazed, cocked his head, and gave that pot a long, cross-eyed stare. He crept closer, still staring, stretched out his neck— and set off a third mousetrap!

That was enough for big, brave Killer. He turned tail, went over to his couch way across the room from the now dangerous gardenia, stared at it a long time, and never rooted in another potted plant.

Now what happens in the Mousetrap Trick is that you get the thing itself to strike back, you see. Killer didn't swear off potted plants because of any advice I gave him; he swore off potted plants because they were obviously dangerous things to fool around with; at any minute they may snap your nose and scare you.

Emboldened by my success with mousetrapping, I branched out into other areas where I wanted my dogs to believe that things themselves fought back. Captain Ahab was particularly bad about removing any tasty little goodies that appealed to him from kitchen counters. A brief fling with mousetraps convinced him that countertops were inherently dangerous. Since then, through the judicious use of mousetraps, I've discouraged another dog, Gemini, from sitting on our dresser to look out the window. Friends have broken their St. Bernard of getting on the couch via the Old Mousetrap Trick. There are endless possibilities. Even better, the lessons learned are learned permanently, not just while we're in sight and sound of the dog.

And are mousetraps actually, as any one of my dogs would claim, dangerous? No! They give off a little snap, and they have very little force. It's the surprise factor that works, as well as the unexpected noise. It's remotely possible that a very tiny puppy might get a foot caught in a mousetrap, but a puppy tiny enough to be hurt by a mousetrap isn't destroying big indoor plants, grazing off your countertops, or sprawling the length of a nine-foot couch. So I doubt you need worry about fractures caused by judicious mousetrapping! Consider, I say, the alternatives.

Chapter 6
Breaking Bad Habits

Besides the challenge of starting a new puppy right with good habits, there's the issue of the older puppy who has developed some bad habits that you need to break. I categorically reject that old saw about not being able to teach an old dog, be it new tricks or new behavior. However, some older puppies need much stronger measures than we'd ever have to use on an inexperienced baby pup. I have seen many cases when correct training methods saved dogs from being killed or abandoned to pounds. Consider Rudy, a German shepherd mix whose owner had been told by the local Animal Control Officer, "Get him trained or prepare to have him put to sleep." Rudy's young owner brought him to my obedience class as her last resort. Used to having his own way and having bitten several people, Rudy was a dog truly out of control. He challenged me at every opportunity, unwilling to give up his alpha dog status. Judy, his owner, had to learn to be the ultimate authority in his life, and she was, understandably, scared of him. But she had heart, and she didn't want her pet to be killed, so she learned her lessons thoroughly. Not only did Rudy graduate from obedience class

with the top score; more important, he never again threatened to bite people. Years later, he was living a fine life with Judy, all because she was willing to go the extra mile to save his life and make a decent dog out of him. So don't despair of breaking bad habits. Just get creative, think the matter through the way a dog would see the situation, and apply solutions. In this chapter you'll meet a couple of my favorite solutions and some that are, indeed, extreme. I hope you won't need radical strategies; but if you find yourself in the kind of predicament Judy was in, using extreme measures correctly will be the kindest thing you'll do for your pup. Most of the strategies in

Some habits are cute, but you may not find it amusing when Puppy sloshes water all over the kitchen floor.

this chapter depend on being able to think like a dog, understand what motivates dogs, and be creative. Some of these training tricks are even fun for you, the harassed human.

Trashpickers

I've had several dogs, as you may have, too, that were positive that I kept throwing good stuff into the trashbasket. Their mission in life was retrieving it. In the process, many of them also decorated the house with what I mistakenly called "trash." Such differences of taste and opinion I find hard to live with.

The most persistent was Bucky, my last weimaraner. In seeking a way to discourage his trashpicking, I found the Ultimate—and it was fun for me! Instead of either making sure there wasn't a scrap in any trashbasket in the house or hiding every trashbasket (going through the rou-

tine I used to call "Bucky-proofing the house"), this day I took a rather full wastebasket into the middle of the kitchen. Removing the contents, I layered the basket: A layer of paper, a generous sprinkling of cayenne; another layer of junk, another generous layer of cayenne, ending with a thin layer of paper. Nearby I placed a very large bucket of water, then I went chuckling off to work. All day I chuckled about Bucky's surprise when he dived into such an easily available trashbasket.

Sure enough, when I got home there was a light sprinkling of chewed paper near the basket, about a third of the water was gone from the bucket, and the rest of the trash was where I thought it belonged—in the basket.

For a change I wasn't angry at Bucky when I got home. I didn't have to go through a major cleanup, didn't have to seethe. It was a fine homecoming for both of us. For several days subsequent to the first, I booby trapped the trashbasket, but never again did Bucky pick through it.

I thoroughly recommend this method. If it cured incorrigible Bucky, it'll cure any habit. It's not cruel; you don't have to strike your dog (which does no good for anything except your frustrations ex post facto, anyway). Nobody gets into a temper, and it's sort of fun to be creative about the booby trapping. Like the Mousetrap Trick, this is a way of getting the thing itself to strike back, which is highly effective training.

A trashpicker at work.

The Hopeless Digger

Having a dog or dogs doesn't have to mean that you must give up all attempts to landscape your yard in a style other than Early Moon Crater. Now I hold that a certain amount of digging seems to be good for a dog's soul and should, hence, be allowed. You already know that I believe a dog should have a pen of her/his own; how that dog landscapes the pen is the dog's business. If holes are what s/he finds aesthetically pleasing, don't quibble—as far as the pen is concerned. But your pen, otherwise known as the rest of the yard, should be landscaped according to your aesthetic leanings. Maybe, like me, you don't lean to huge craters in what you laughingly call a lawn. Over the years, I've heard from many people who were at their wits' end as far as maintaining any sort of yard and shrubbery was concerned. Let us suppose that you have either a stubborn dog, a hunting breed, or an enthusiastic terrier. In other words, you have a world-class digger! No amount of yelling, scolding, or jumping up and down has prevented continual excavation. You've tried the supposedly sure method of squirting the digger with water from a hose, and that hasn't worked. You've used the no-dig chemicals, touted for discouraging digging, and they haven't worked. A remedy exists.

Heidi was an enthusiastic gopher-trailer. When she was after a gopher, she could do more damage to a lawn in three minutes than a whole convention of gophers could do in three years. She dug so furiously that once I saw her throw the gopher backwards out of its hole and over her head without even realizing that she'd overshot her quarry.

One issue of the weimaraner magazine carried the suggestion that to discourage digging, one should catch the dog in full dig, take a hose and fill the hole with water. This step will discourage 99 percent of the diggers. For that remaining hopeless one percent, go on to step 2: Grab the dog by the collar and stick its head under water in the hole for a second or two.

I caught Heidi digging (this wasn't something I had to wait around for very long!) and followed instructions. She struggled, and I let her surface. She ran to the house, giving up all idea of getting her gopher. After

Your puppy is not the one to decide how you want your yard landscaped.

several episodes of water-filled holes on the lawn, she learned that the yard proper was off limits for digging. Later in her life when we moved to a new place, all I had to do was say, "Heidi, no" when she began to dig off limits and she'd quit. So the method works and has carry-over. Thus far I haven't needed this method with Danes, as they're more attuned to voice control and not such avid hunters, but I know people with terriers to whom I've suggested the water method, and they report it works. Set yourself up in advance by having a hose with a drip-proof nozzle easily accessible in your yard. Leave the water to the hose turned on, so all you have to do is grab the digger with one hand and turn the nozzle on with the other. Speed and surprise are critical here.

Your dog isn't going to like this correction and will struggle. You'll be smart enough to hold her/his nose underwater very briefly the first time, a little longer should a second time be necessary, and even longer if repeats are needed. *(But please be sure not to overdo it!)* While you're doing this, say loudly, "NO DIG!" What you want from this correction is what you want from any correction—to replace a physical correction with a vocal one as soon as your dog has the message.

What you always want is a dog you can love and live with, not some semi-wild creature that is a torment to you every day of your life. You're teaching your dog to live in your pack and to follow the pack rules.

I can't repeat often enough—the animal shelters and dog pounds are full of abandoned dogs that no one cared for enough to teach them the rules.

Tin Pan Alley

I owned my first weimaraner, Blitzkrieg, in Connecticut many years ago. He and I lived in a country house near a woods that was the last big shelter wild animals had, what with suburban sprawl. For a hunting dog, this place was ideal. However, in Connecticut at that time, there was absolutely no deer season. The real stinger in the "no deer hunting" law was that if a game warden caught your dog off by itself independently hunting deer, even if the dog had no gun, the warden was legally empowered to shoot the dog. Thus it was important not only for the sake of the deer, but also for the

The "tin pan alley" technique can help you teach your dog to stay within unfenced boundaries.

sake of the dog that I not allow him to hunt deer.

Yet deer wandered right through our front yard—tame, lovely creatures that I liked to watch and liked to have around. One day as I was watching, Blitz came from the backyard where he'd been mulching around, put his nose to the ground, and was off following the deer that had just gone into the woods. Fortunately for both of us, he was well enough trained to come back at my call, but he came reluctantly. Later the same day, we were both out in the yard, and, true to his nature, Blitz took the deer trail again.

I inquired among dog knowledgeable friends, and this is the remedy that worked: The next day, when again Blitz took a deer trail, I came boiling out of the house armed with two large metal pie pans. I proceeded to beat them together, jumping up and down, shouting and yodeling and making an enormous ruckus.

Blitz was astounded.

As soon as I was sure I had his undivided attention, I took his collar, pointed to the deer trail and gave a most firm NO, then took him into the house with me.

I had to repeat this procedure for three days. On the fourth day I saw deer go through the front yard in the early morning. About half an hour later, with the trail still very fresh, I let Blitz out. From a window I watched as he put his nose to the trail, sniffed, then picked up his head and gave a look of utter disgust, whereupon he walked away from the deer trail and began working on woodchucks.

That was the end of Blitz's interest in deer.

I might add that this method of banging pie pans and yelling is marvelous for getting out our hostilities and frustrations—really lots of fun if you let yourself go and get into the spirit of the thing. It doesn't much matter what you yell as long as lots of NOs are liberally sprinkled in.

I've since used this method to discourage dogs from leaving the confines of their property or going out into the street. I know a fence is probably better because it's surer, but I like knowing that fence or no fence, my dogs won't go off limits.

Incidentally, this tactic seems not to work on cats; I've experimented. It just scares them so badly that their brains turn to mush and they learn nothing.

The Balkan Question

If you're the kind of person who believes a dog lives outdoors and never has access to your living quarters, we are not on the same wavelength. Why anyone would expect a dog to "watch" a house s/he has no stake in is beyond me. My neighbor, in fact, is a fine example of someone who does not know how a dog thinks. The man bought a golden retriever mixed-breed dog, which he chains to a doghouse in the far back

This eleven-week-old sharpei seems to understand that she is the guardian of house and yard.

of his property "to watch the place," as the man explained it to me. Well, all the poor dog can do is watch, as its chain is too short to allow it to get close to the house, and it's never off that chain. After a thief broke into the house, my neighbor was convinced that he'd gotten a dog of inferior intelligence!

Anyway, if you're interested in civilizing your puppy, you most likely also share your house with your dog. My tastes are that we share almost all the house most of the time. The dining room is often off limits, and sometimes the bedrooms are. When it rains in Humboldt County and our world turns to mud, dogs stay in the kitchen until their feet are dry. But how do we impart to whatever dogs are in the house just what the current boundaries are?

Insurmountable Obstacles

The answer is very simple: We train all our dogs from puppyhood to know that a baby gate is an insurmountable obstacle. There are many types of baby gates, from the old-fashioned, folding wooden ones that I still use to high-tech, high-priced affairs that slide aside when they're not needed. If you have a little dog that could scoot through the holes in the wooden gates, one of the mesh gates is preferable. Then, keep baby gates at any door through which you may not want a dog to pass.

When I'm raising a litter of puppies, I use a gate to bar exits from the kitchen. One room of potential chaos is all I'm up to. For the first few weeks a board about eight inches high has to be propped between the gate and the door frame, as the pups are small enough to scoot between the interstices of the gate.

Whenever one of us leaves the kitchen, we close the gate and tell the puppies, "You STAY." Depending on the pups, there's more or less whining and fussing. If they're really obnoxious, out come the water pistols and we begin that lesson, too. What's happening is that the pups are casually learning several things at once: To respect confining boundaries; to hear the "Stay" command; to know "NO" (which they sort of know already, having heard that word in connection with trying to chew on our fingers while still in the puppy box); and to realize that fussing isn't going to do them any good as far as making us change our minds.

When we return to the kitchen, we make a point of greeting the puppies as gladly as they greet us.

Thus another lesson is building: We go away, but we come back and are glad to see them when we do.

Soon the board can go back to storage. Not only may the pups be too big to slip through the gate, but more important, they know now that the closed gate means that they must stay where they are. Occasionally we have escape artists. The remedy for that is simply an instantaneous return to the kitchen. I find it generally unnecessary even to scold; just put the puppy back and repeat the commands. The more hardheaded breeds may need considerably more water-pistol persuasion to teach them that the gate means what you say it means.

By the time pups graduate to the living room with us, there are gates across the dining room and bedroom doors—one room at a time, as 'twere, and eventually, we share the entire house with our dogs. Delightfully, though, young pups are so used to baby gates as obstacles that they don't try to get into the gated-off rooms. Once a puppy learns the theory of what baby gates mean, s/he respects the barrier quality of all baby gates. Gating works very well when we have—as we often do—puppies as well as a big male who may not be too crazy about puppies in the house. The adult dog can go into the bedroom and be safe while still being in the house. Or if we have one bitch in the house, and we want to bring another in, and need time for the two of them to remember that they do, too, get

along, we just put up a gate to gain that time. Or if you have an older dog who is having trouble accepting the new puppy, use of gates makes the get-acquainted period smoother.

Obviously no baby gate is going to hold back a large dog who wants to go through it. I remember with amusement the day I put a gate across the den door with Cappy behind the gate and went to answer the front door. As I was letting my friend in, I got a nudge from a Dane nose, and there was Cappy, wearing what was left of the gate. I'd forgotten that I hadn't trained him to a gate, and he was wondering why he had to wear this funny new collar. Yet in a few days, Cappy knew about gates. He'd do his little dance behind the gate and sing his little song, but he wouldn't come through.

The baby gate becomes an insurmountable obstacle—and your puppy is safe where you put it.

Protection for Everyone

People who love dogs generally have very few guests who don't like dogs—for obvious reasons. But sometimes if we're having a party,

us have large dogs is that we value their protective natures, and we all know dozens of stories about faithful family defenders in the canine world. I have seldom known a dog to take an unwarranted dislike to someone.

Besides reserving our own space, we humans owe it to our dogs to let them also have their own space when they're sick of us or of our guests. This is where crates come into everyone's life. You know all about those from Chapter 3, so I need not deal further with that aid to dog and human sanity.

it's nice for us not to have the dogs monopolizing the living room, so again the gates come into good use. Many dogs take a dislike to certain people. One neighbor incurred dislike the first time he met Caesar by taking off his hat and swatting Caesar with it. Caesar never forgave Lee that breach of manners; I could always tell that it was Lee at the door, because Caesar snarled as he did at no other visitor. I'd quickly tell Lee, "Just a minute," and put Caesar in the bedroom behind the gate. Such a flimsy barrier, but Caesar knew I didn't want him to bite Lee, and being behind the gate saved Caesar's self-respect: He would bite Lee if he could, but being so hopelessly confined, don't you see, he could do nothing but accept his position. Lee was, incidentally, told of his breach and advised to stay away from the bedroom door.

Of course, should the situation warrant, any dog we have would come right through a baby gate to defend either Kent or me, and we all know it. One of the reasons many of

Meeting Strangers

Although I get testy when people use that false cliche "It's a dog eat dog world," (Have you ever *seen* a dog eat another dog? Of course not!) I'm painfully aware that it *is* all too often a "dog bite dog world." Think like a dog for a minute here. You, faithful protector of your person, are out walking your human. You are minding your business, which is the safety and well-being of your human. Suddenly a strange dog rushes toward the two of you! This is a threat to your person, so you bristle and give a warning growl. But the approaching dog ignores you and comes on.

There's only one response a self-respecting dog can possibly make: You snap at the stranger. If the stranger has a shred of sense, it backs off, and you can continue your walk in peace. But not all dogs have sense, and some strangers have to be forcefully taught to stay away. Suddenly, you find yourself in the middle of a nasty fight that you never looked for.

That's how a dog sees it when a strange dog invades the sacred space around it and its person. That's why dogfights happen.

That's also why you absolutely *must* leash your dog when you're in places where strange dogs are around. One of the problems that I see many times on Internet discussions of canine behavior is what to do when an unleashed dog rushes up to you and your leashed dog while you're out for a walk.

First, be careful where you walk with your dog until you're sure that you have control of your pet. If your dog still lunges for other dogs even when it's on leash, you've got to work hard on the verbal and physical commands to break that lunging. This is where a strong chain choker is useful, and, in extreme cases, even a prong collar. The shock of a snapped choker coupled with your sharp and loud NO will change your dog's mind about lunging at other dogs.

But what if your dog is well-mannered, heels just fine, and a loose dog comes rushing up?

This is when all your alpha dog training comes to your rescue. You must become the biggest, baddest dog in the neighborhood. Your NOs must echo. Every nuance of your body language must shout, "Don't mess with me!" Your voice must be the voice of authority. Every lesson you ever got on being nice must go out the window! You may have to kick. You surely will have to shout.

And you owe no politeness to whatever lout of an owner comes strolling up blathering about, "Oh, my dog is just fine. He loves all the other little doggies." When you can muster some replica of a human voice, speak of leash laws and local ordinances about out-of-control dogs and other such details that this creep is disregarding.

We all should be able to go for nice walks with our dogs and not have to fear attack. Every one of us has to do our part to make this situation be so. That includes never taking your dog off leash anywhere public until you know beyond any doubt that your dog will respond to your COME command faster than a speeding bullet. And it also includes being alert for trouble signs.

Some breeds are, of course, more protective and territorial than others. You've got to know your breed. Terriers are notorious for being ready to take on every dog in the world. I'll never forget the class of sixteen standard schnauzer bitches at a show in Santa Barbara. One of the bitches broke and attacked the bitch in front of her. Before anyone could react, all sixteen schnauzers were a whirlwind of fangs and snarls. Even the judge had to get in on the grabbing, kicking, and hauling that eventually broke up the melee. The class went on, apparently serenely, and every one of those bitches looked just gorgeous because they were all "up" and spirited.

But what you'd really liked to have seen were all the Dane owners and the Saint owners, for our dogs were due in the ring the schnauzers were soon to vacate and the ring next to it. There were perhaps eighty of the giant dogs gathered for their day of glory when the schnauzers got into it. Eighty or more humans quietly, firmly, slowly faded their dogs from the scene, making sure that every dog's nose was where it ought to be and that no dog was commenting on what fun the schnauzer fight looked to be.

Had that gang broken, we'd have had to call in the Marines!

Walk on Water

One of the greatest things about imaginative dog training is that, using the right tools, you can convince your dog that you doubtless could, if you wanted to, walk on water. Here are some more tricks you can use to control a puppy or dog that thinks it's out of your reach and thus out of your control.

Water Pistols

There may be some people who outgrow their childhood delight in playing with water pistols. I am not one of these. Therefore, it was perhaps inevitable that I discovered years ago that a water pistol I had confiscated from one of my high school students was a very effective weapon against a weimaraner puppy whose mischief was getting me out of my chair so often that I resembled a human yo-yo. The water-pistol technique, refined, consists of timing things so that one's sharp "NO!" hits the puppy's ears at the same instant that the squirt of water lands from across the room. To the pup, this double whammy is amazing. There you are, still seated in your chair and supposedly unable to touch him/her from such a distance, yet there's a distinct wet spot that says you have touched! Because you haven't moved, gone is the game of See If Owner Can Catch Puppy, which eliminates much of the fun of being naughty for a pup. Needless to say, for a person who has other things to do all day besides chase a puppy around, the water pistol method of civilizing is a real energy saver. And, unlike the thrown object, the stream of water doesn't have to be retrieved.

The Big Guns

Working up somewhat from water pistols, I used the water method to save the lives of three of my dogs. This is another of the zany training tactics you may need at some time in your life with canines. At the time I lived on a ranch of which mine was the first house; the main ranch house was further up our shared driveway. Dutch and Mary, who lived in the main house, had lots of guests, many of whom drove that dirt lane as if training for the Grand Prix. For dogs that stayed in their own yard, the driveway posed no threat. However, my young male weimaraner—the infamous Bucky—took to loping off after every car going up to the main house. Not to be outdone, Heidi, his mother, and Sapphire, my black Dane bitch, joined in the chase, vying with each other to see who could bring home the biggest car as a trophy. My running after them only added to the total hilarity of the situation and sped them in their pursuit. Were they asking each other who could outrun me the best? Or did they believe I, too, was chasing cars? No matter. The situation was, literally, out of hand. The unimaginative thing to do was pen them up—always. That didn't appeal to me, as it would deprive me of the pleasure of the dogs' company when I was out in the yard.

So I invited several friends for a picnic. Instructions were for each person to bring a car and some water-spouting weapon. After supper, festivities began. My friends tore up and down the driveway in their cars, gleefully squirting the dogs with an arsenal of water pistols, plant sprayers, and what-have-yous. Four passes it took. On the fifth, as the sound of cars drew nigh, all three dogs turned tail and beat it to the front door, demanding that I let them in and save their lives from such mayhem. We humans tried a few more jaunts up and down the driveway, sometimes squirting each other in the absence of dogs, but the dogs were cured of their car chasing, and no one could get the slightest chase out of them.

Just simple, clean, cold water was all it took, plus a little imagination and a few nutty friends who enjoyed helping out. As a result, three dogs who could have been either killed or banished to pens for life became fine, sensible canines who let cars pass unchallenged for the rest of their lives. I'm happy to say that the lesson learned that day carried over; wherever we four lived for the rest of the dogs' lives, no car ever got chased again.

The Shakedown

If you've watched bitches with their puppies, you've seen an exasperated mother pick up an unruly pup and shake it. This is not only a correction to the pup, it's a humiliation. The shakedown makes very clear to the puppy who is the boss. Generally after having been shaken, a puppy will roll over on its back and put its legs in the air. This position is a way of saying, "Okay. I know I'm low dog on the ladder, and here I am showing you how submissive I am." Few puppies repeat behavior for which their mothers have shaken them. They've learned their first lesson about alpha dogs.

There are extreme cases in which people have to use the shakedown to establish their alpha status with an incorrigible dog. I learned the shakedown technique with—you guessed it, Bucky! He was unwilling to accord me alpha status and pushed his limits. Again the weimaraner magazine came to my aid, detailing the technique of picking your dog up by the loose skin of its back and neck, shaking it, and dropping it to the ground. Well, picking up a full-grown weimaraner seemed like an enterprise I wasn't up to, and only under the most severe provocation did I resort to it. A friend was visiting with his champion corgi, whom Bucky didn't like. True, the corgi was a little pest, harassing Bucky and then slipping out of reach, but I insist that a big dog not pick on a little one, and I'm against dogs' fighting in general. The corgi snipped at Bucky, and this time, it didn't run fast enough. Bucky lunged for it. I lunged for Bucky, and the next thing I knew, I had all four of Bucky's feet off the ground and I was shaking him. Dropping him to the ground, I uttered the expletive the magazine had suggested: Pfui! To my surprise, Bucky stayed crouched where I'd tossed him and made no further moves toward the corgi. My friend and I leashed both dogs and cut our afternoon walk short, each dog subdued by the display of my alpha behavior.

I won't go so far as to say that forever more Bucky did everything I wanted him to do, but he did respect me more. I, too, had greater confidence in myself as his leader, though

Mixed breed pups can be fine pets, but often you have to guess what their temperament and intelligence will be.

I didn't repeat the shakedown. Surprisingly, the "Pfui!" reminded him of my utter disgust with unacceptable behavior and became a powerful command to get his attention.

A friend who raises dalmatians uses the shakedown fairly regularly, and it's obvious that in his pack, he's respected as the alpha. Other friends who have terriers also do periodic shakedowns, especially if they're quieting down behavior that could be preliminary to a general all-out terrier scrap.

One uses the shakedown *only* to interrupt hideously unacceptable behavior, and with smaller dogs, one must be careful about dropping the dog to the ground so you don't injure it. Consider the shakedown as a kind of last resort, and something you may never have to do. Understand that you're giving your dog a major humiliation if you use the shakedown, and use it, if at all, only in extreme situations for behavior you need to interrupt. I emphasize this because the shakedown overused can break your dog's spirit and make it wary of you rather than respectful. Shakedowns and similar corrections should be used very cautiously with dogs showing dominance aggression.

Fortunately, whoever set the standards for the really giant breeds' temperaments was wise enough to breed dogs that want to please their owners. In more than a quarter century with Danes, never have I even come close to needing a shakedown in our Dane family.

Chapter 7
Cleaning Up

An often overlooked aspect of civilizing a puppy is getting and keeping him or her groomed. Especially when you think of a puppy as an integral member of your family, you want the canine member to be as clean as anyone else in the house. Although my first criterion when considering what dog I want is the temperament of the breed, grooming and the amount of time that must be invested is a close second. Recently I was sorely tempted by a cocker spaniel puppy offered to me by friends who breed cockers. He was everything a cocker should be: outgoing, of a sunny disposition, alert but not hyper, and just beautifully put together. I came very close to adding him to our family—until I thought seriously about the grooming he truly deserved; I faced the fact that boxers, then weimaraners, and finally Danes have spoiled me with their smooth coats and easy grooming. That cocker puppy needs and deserves daily brushing, and I'm unlikely to provide it.

So add to the list of qualities you want in dogs the level of grooming you're able and willing to do. People ought, I believe, to be brutally honest with themselves when they're dreaming of owning their ideal dog. Even if one can afford weekly trips to the grooming shop for a dog, there is still the daily upkeep that every dog deserves. A matted, dirty dog is an unhappy dog, and its owner does it a disservice keeping it in such shabby condition. A vital part of its civilizing process is neglected.

Brushing

For any dogs, except the smooth-haired ones like boxers and Italian greyhounds, a daily brushing is the key to good grooming. Brushing is

Always ready to cooperate!

far more important than bathing, and is good for your dog's coat and skin, as too frequent bathing is not. Depending on how heavily coated your dog is, daily brushing takes from a few minutes to an hour. A wire brush gets out the tangles before they become mats, and also gets rid of dead hair. Brushing the dog daily keeps your carpets free of clouds of dog hair and allows you to wear something other than tweedy clothes that disguise the dog hair! My friend Ken was busy and didn't brush his chow for a few days. When it came time to clean house, Ken had to use a rake to gather up his dog's contributions to the decor. He said ruefully that brushing his dog actually takes less time than cleaning up from not doing so.

Not only does the daily brushing keep the dog hair from accumulating in the house, it also gets rid of loose dirt on the dog. A quick brushing after you and your dog come back from a walk by the river or a trek through the woods will remove any debris the dog has picked up. More important, brushing before you both come into the house will let you check your pup for ticks. You may even see tiny ticks that haven't yet attached themselves to the pup and you'll dislodge those that aren't firmly latched on.

Start gently and regularly brushing your puppy, doing it often but not necessarily for long periods at a time, and you'll end up with an adult dog who just loves to be brushed. Be careful not to pull at tangles. Clip mats instead of yanking them. Do brush the puppy's feet, even though they may seem not to need much attention. This kind of gentle, non-threatening handling of the feet prepares a puppy for having its nails trimmed. Once convinced that you're not going to hurt its feet, Puppy is less likely to go ballistic when you bring out the nail clippers. The dog who has been gently and lovingly brushed responds happily to the sight of its brush and appreciates grooming sessions as times of close bonding and companionship with its person.

Even for smooth-haired dogs, brushing after walks is helpful for tick and debris removal. It's beneficial, too, spring and fall at shedding season. It is astonishing how much tiny white hair a dog like a harlequin Dane can drop around the house when

Daily brushing is the key to good grooming.

shedding. With a smooth-haired dog, one uses a bristle brush or a grooming mitt rather than the wire brush. Black or blue Danes can get very ugly when they're shedding—or, as it's called, "blowing" coat. The dead hair turns dull and brownish, and you wonder what's happening to your dog. Once upon a time I was so appalled at how Jezebel, a black bitch we bought, looked when she was blowing coat that I called knowledgeable Dane friends.

"That black bitch I bought in Oregon," I began hesitantly.

"Yes?" my friend asked, hearing the unease in my voice.

"She couldn't be really a chocolate, could she?" I was truly worried, as we had bought Jezebel to be part of our breeding program and I assure you that so-called chocolate Danes are not on any Dane breeder's wish list!

Over the phone lines came my friend's cackling laughter.

It's not funny," I snapped, cranky now because I thought she was laughing at me for having been taken.

When she could stop laughing, she informed me that what I was seeing was very common in black Danes, especially young ones, when they blew their winter coats. "Rusty spots?" she asked me. "Brownish hair in patches?"

Oh, I was seeing all that, indeed I was.

"Get an old, very dull hacksaw blade," my friend counseled me, "and use it as you would a comb. That will hasten the shedding process. I assure you, Jezebel's breeder is impeccably ethical. You do not have a chocolate Dane."

My friend Eileen was right; I had a fine, properly bred black Dane bitch, and in years to come I saw lots of ugly spring coats, wore out many dull, old hacksaw blades, and came to laugh at my early consternation about black Danes turning chocolate. But if you're seeing change in your puppy's coloring at shedding time, before you hit the panic button, get busy on grooming.

Skip the old hacksaw blade makeshift. Get a stripping comb at your local pet shop and start stripping. You'll be surprised at how much hair will drift off your pup—dead, discolored hair that looks awful; it itches, to boot.

Towel-on Cleansers

Along with frequent brushing, various liquid dog cleansing products readily available at pet stores and pet counters aid in keeping your pup clean and smelling good. Most major pet product companies have this grooming aid, selling them under names like Skip Bath. Products I've used smell good and do what they promise, which is to freshen up your pup when a bath isn't practical. I first learned of these when we had cockers who liked nothing better than to find something loathsomely smelly in the fields and roll in it. A brisk toweling with one of the bath substitutes, the reeking spot was gone, and we had a dog who could reasonably join polite human society.

On smooth-coated dogs, the product cleans them up in no time, keeps you from having to give baths when the weather's cold, and is great for a dog that's not feeling well but needs freshening up.

Hold the Soap and Water

Frequent bathing is bad for dogs and possibly fatal for puppies. A young puppy born in winter months is going to get messy, and your temptation is to bathe it. Don't! Try one of the products I've just mentioned, and keep the puppy warm during and after the process. Pups get chilled very easily, and puppy chills tend to lead to illness and debilitation. During inclement weather, brush Puppy a lot, use bath substitutes, and maybe even do some spot cleaning. But hold off on the bathing until Puppy is older and the weather is warmer. The more heavily coated Puppy is, the longer it's going to take to get her/him dry and warm again.

Bathing destroys the natural oils on a dog's skin and dries the coat. We truly do not bathe some Danes from one year to the next, even though they live in the house with us and share a lot of the furniture. Brisk brushing, use of bath substitutes, and keeping them in clean kennels and sleeping quarters is the proper regime for any of the smooth-coated dogs. Sometimes, if a dog is losing a lot of coat, a bath will speed up the shedding process, though you'll be faced with drifts of dog hair for a couple of days after the bath.

Teaching your puppy about bath time is important. The water should be little more than lukewarm, and it should be shallow enough that the pup isn't afraid of drowning. Good footing in the bathtub or sink is important so Puppy isn't afraid of falling. If your bathtub doesn't have nonskid strips, get some and apply them. Your manner throughout the process needs to be reassuringly cheerful; this is a new experience for Puppy, and one that's potentially threatening. Be careful not to get soap in the puppy's eyes, and don't deluge its ears with water.

The TUB Command—For Dogs That Don't Fit in Sinks!

If yours is going to be a giant in adulthood like mine are, begin to teach the TUB! command before you actually want to do a major bath. This is stuff you need to teach fairly early—say at six months or so, because there will soon come a tim when you will not physically be able to pick Puppy up and plop him/her into the bathtub. Begin by enticing your adolescent puppy into the empty bathtub with treats. Once it's in the tub, pet the puppy, reassure it, and make it SIT and STAY. One of the things you want least in life is a big, wet dog leaping out of the tub and shaking in the bathroom!

Keep at the TUB! command and rewards for getting into an empty bathtub until Puppy willingly steps into the bathtub on command. Then put a little warm water in the tub, repeating the command. Bit by bit, you'll teach Puppy that hopping into a bathtub of water and staying there calmly throughout a bath is no big deal, and you'll congratulate yourself for years to come on having been so foresighted.

A tub plumbed with a shower spray is excellent for rinsing dogs. Dogs seem not to like noisy running water in their tubs, so the spray quiets that problem. More important, soap left on a dog's coat really dulls it and encourages itchy, flaky skin, so thorough rinsing is necessary. The spray does that very well.

Lacking a spray, use a dipper of some sort to pour water over your dog until its coat is literally squeaky clean. As you change from the soapy bathwater to the clear rinse water, be careful to keep the temperature on the cool side. Hot water could scald.

Your carefully trained dog will sit or stand/stay through all this, and

If you have a really large dog, you'll be glad you taught the TUB! command.

not until you give the okay will it step daintily out of the tub, where you will have the biggest towel you own ready to wrap the dog in before it gives a nice big natural shake and deluges you and the entire room with water.

Depending on how much dog you have to dry, you'll go through a lot of towels (or all the towels in the house!). With a coated dog, you'll probably end up using a hair dryer, too.

Your dog will now insist it has to go out. This is not the time! Most dogs will go directly from the bath to the dirtiest spot they can find and roll, instantly undoing all your good work. If you really believe the OUT request, make it an outing on leash where you have control. And make it brief so your dog doesn't get chilly.

Skunked!

Bucky, fine weimaraner that he was, knew better than to hassle a skunk. But at the time we also had a feisty, delightful little terrier-beagle cross named Charlie who adored Bucky, aped him, and tempted him into foolishness he'd have avoided had he not had his little admirer egging him on. So it was inevitable, given Charlie's beagle hunting instincts coupled with his terrier rashness, that he'd find a skunk in our woods and be too small to do anything useful about the varmint. What Charlie did was dance around Bucky, gleefully yapping as Bucky tried to stare the skunk out of existence. Perhaps rattled by Charlie's insistence that something be done about the skunk, Bucky grabbed it by the neck and killed it, though not before getting thoroughly sprayed. A stinky, crestfallen Bucky showed up on the porch, followed closely by a happy, bouncy, equally stinky Charlie.

No one wants to live with a skunkstinky dog, and no one has to. Though there are many products on the market that claim to get rid of skunk smell, none in my experience works as well as the time-tested remedy of canned stewed tomatoes. Not tomato juice, as some recommend, but actual stewed tomatoes. You need the chunks of tomato to rub stubborn spots of smell out. Scrub your skunky dog well with the tomatoes and then bathe the dog as usual. It's not necessary to let the tomatoes dry on the dog's coat, nor is it necessary, as some claim, to leave the dog overnight with tomatoes on its coat. I have had to repeat the tomato scrub and give a second bath, but that was with a dog (well,

yes, Blitz, another weimaraner) who was due in the ring at the big two-day Boston benched show the next morning at ten o'clock. Understandably, I wanted to make certain that no lingering aroma followed us around the ring!

And, lest weimaraners get stuck with an unfair reputation for stupidity where skunks are concerned, we've also had Danes that would not abide live skunks on their premises. Some were fast and smart enough not to get sprayed, some weren't. But just in case, I strongly recommend that in your Emergency Dog Supply Department you keep a very large can of stewed tomatoes. If you're really lucky, your dog will grow old and sensible and you can eat the tomatoes. It does tend to be the young dogs who can't bear to leave well enough alone.

And, yes, I scrubbed Charlie, too—though for his troublemaking, I made him wait until Bucky was all cleaned up.

Toenails

Especially if you've just given your dog a bath and its nails are softened, this is a fine time to clip toenails. However, nails need to be clipped more often than a dog needs to be bathed, so don't wait only for bath time to do this vital maintenance job.

Most dogs don't like to have their toenails clipped. Some, in fact, fight the process mightily. Often a dog that fights having its nails clipped was at some time hurt during the process, and this is, unfortunately, easy to do. Blood vessels in a dog's toenails come very close to the end of the nail. You can see the blood vessels in a dog that has clear nails; they are harder to spot if the dog has dark or black nails. What you want to do in clipping nails is to snip off only the dead part of the nail that protrudes beyond the blood vessel, or "quick." This dead part is a different color than the living nail.

This is another of those grooming duties that you'd do well to start as early as possible with your puppy. Using regular toenail clippers for humans, snip off the sharp ends of the baby puppies' nails while they're still nursing, as those sharp little nails are hard on Mom. Carefully take only the tips of the nails; the puppies don't get hurt because you're not hitting the quick ("quicking").

Soon toenail clippers aren't strong enough to do pups' nails. Move on to the specially made dog toenail clippers. Again, be careful not to quick them, but squirmy pups can get quicked, so keep styptic powder handy to stanch the bleeding, as a remarkable amount of bleeding can occur. I'm more conservative in doing nails than Kent is, often not even taking off enough in my zeal not to quick anyone. I broadcast my uneasiness at the process, and soon our dogs know they can bamboozle me into abbreviating nail clipping, whereas with Kent, they flop out on their sides and

Trimming a dog's nails. Hold the clippers at an angle and avoid cutting the quick.

offer him one paw at a time, all the while rolling their eyes at their amazing martyrdom. Not everyone in a family is equally good at every aspect of puppy training or grooming. If you realize you're broadcasting your uneasiness at something like nail clipping, see whether some other family member may be better suited to the task.

If you don't know how to clip your puppy's nails, get someone to walk you through it once or twice—the breeder you got Puppy from, your vet, or a groomer. And if you have a puppy that's going to need professional grooming regularly, you may choose never to know how to clip toenails and just leave it to the groomer.

But toenails must be kept short. We've seen little dogs with nails recurving back into their pads, hobbling about because their feet hurt from neglected toenails. On bigger dogs, neglected toenails often result in splayed and otherwise deformed feet. It is difficult for a dog to walk properly if its toenails are so long that the pads of its feet aren't making contact with the surface. The ideal

Use a cotton swab gently. Never probe inside the ear canal!

is that you don't hear the click of toenails when your pup walks across a bare wood or linoleum floor.

Dogs that dig a lot wear down their own front nails. Running on sand is very good for wearing down toenails. Walking on concrete pavement also keeps nails in trim. But

This is what the inside of your pup's ear looks like—1. pinna, 2. vertical canal, 3. horizontal canal, 4. auditory nerves, 5. eardrum.

your average inside city dog that gets little time to run on beaches or dig for gophers is going to need human intervention to have good nails.

Ears

After bathing is a good time to clean your pup's ears, too. Use cotton swabs just as you do for yourself, and be as careful as you are with yourself not to puncture an eardrum. If your puppy is a squirmer, use cotton balls instead of swabs. With those, you're not ever likely to damage the ears. Gently clean out accumulated dirt and wax, leaving a soft, pliable surface.

Ears, like nails, need to be cleaned more often than dogs need to be bathed. Witch hazel or rubbing alcohol are safe and effective products to use to clean your dog's ears. If you want to go beyond these old standards, ask your vet what to use.

If you see your puppy shaking its ears, examine them carefully. Various grasses, especially foxtails, get lodged in dogs' ears and need to be removed. If you can find no reason for the ear shaking, a trip to the vet's for a microscopic check is in order. Especially if you have a cat (or cats) as well as Puppy, there may be ear mites in the family, and these are too small to see with the naked eye. They're also fairly easy to get rid of, though persistence is required. I'd recommend using whatever your vet prescribes rather than some over-the-counter product.

Most dogs love having their ears cleaned, so you can be a hero and do a good deed all at the same time. However, if there's a foul-smelling buildup in the ears or if the ears are inflamed, don't clean them yourself. Get your vet to check so you know what's causing this unhealthy condition and can cure it.

Anal Glands

Dogs have a pair of glands located at either side of the anus that are used for scent-marking their territory. When a dog is very stressed or suddenly unpleasantly surprised, it sometimes reacts by voiding the anal glands. That this has happened becomes clear because this process emits one of the most unpleasant odors you'll ever encounter. For many dogs, that's all you'll ever have to know about these glands, and even that will simply be something you might add to your own stock of Trivial Pursuit questions.

However, there are dogs that have a tendency for their anal glands to become plugged. In smooth-haired dogs, you can tell that the anals are plugged by seeing unusual puffiness around the dog's anus. If a dog is dragging it rear end along the ground, it is likely to have plugged anals (not, as some think, worms). Sometimes the dog has an occasional foul smell, and other dogs exhibit discomfort moving their bowels. Plugged

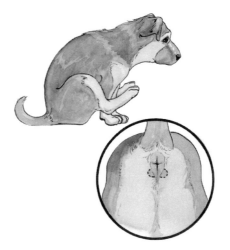

Dragging along the ground is often a sign of plugged anals. The detail shows swollen anal glands.

anals, untreated, become infected, and ultimately this condition can be a lot of big trouble for your dog, so if you have any reason to suspect that your dog's anal glands are plugged, ask your vet to check them for you.

Because Kent and I generally have a lot of dogs, our vet George suggested that I ought to learn to check on and clean our dogs' anal glands myself. George was an excellent teacher, and I'm very good at noticing plugged anal glands and at cleaning them. It's a tricky and potentially smelly job. If you have only one or two dogs and little inclination to get into a job that your dog will not like, leave this maintenance task to your vet. If there should be a reason for you to have to know how to do this, your vet is the one to teach you. You do have to know that there's a potential for problems, though, because prepared is always better.

Teeth

As I said in Chapter 2, I've become convinced that good dental hygiene is as important to our puppies and dogs as it is to us. Therefore, part of the daily care of every puppy should be having its teeth brushed. If there's one part of grooming that needs to be started early, brushing Puppy's teeth is it. Set the good habit from the start and you won't have to fight bad habits.

Like everything else, make the process as much fun for Puppy as you can. Be cheerful, even when Puppy is squirming and claiming it prefers every other brand of toothpaste to the one *your* vet gave it! Get one of the canine toothbrushes that fit over your finger. This kind is easier to grip. Begin with the "easy" teeth, the front ones, and work your way back. As you brush, assure your puppy that s/he's the best puppy in the world. Your cheerful chatter makes the brushing a time of bonding between you and Puppy. As with all other early training, plan on several short sessions at the beginning. Don't insist on perfection at every brushing session right from the start. For one thing, you're working on puppy teeth that are going to fall out anyway, so if you miss a few, so what? But aim for the level of perfection you feel is important, so that by the time Puppy has adult teeth, you're getting them all brushed on a daily basis. Not only are you doing Puppy a favor by taking care of his/her teeth, you're also teaching a vital lesson: That your hands and fingers belong inside Puppy's mouth whenever you choose. This tolerance of your hands in her/his mouth is important when, in the future, you might have to give Puppy pills. It's potentially lifesaving should you need to take something that could be fatal out of Puppy's mouth.

Everything you teach your pup about good grooming today will pay both of you enormous bonuses through your years together. A clean, well-brushed, cooperative dog that enjoys being handled has a drastically better chance at a long, healthy life than does some poor, flea-ridden, matted canine with dirty, rotted teeth and toenails that curve back into its pads.

And though the grooming process takes time, it's good quality time, time when you and your dog can talk over the day's injustices and solve the world's problems.

Clean, healthy teeth don't just happen.

Chapter 8
This and That

Increasing the Vocabulary

Initially, you restrict Puppy's vocabulary, using only a few simple commands so s/he learns the important stuff like NO, OFF, GO POTTY, and COME, with few distractions. You add words like GENTLE as it becomes obvious that Puppy listens to you. Soon you may notice that Puppy is reacting to words you didn't consciously teach, trigger words that elicit certain behavior. One of the first trigger words our dogs seem to pick up is the word GO, as in Kent's asking me whether I plan to GO to town. When every dog in the house wakes up immediately and turns up at the door with an expectant expression, we know that the new puppy has learned that GO always means fun times. I tell you truly, it matters not where I ask my dogs if they want to GO. I've had dogs volunteer for the dump, the moon, and hell—all equally eagerly.

Once a puppy is picking up trigger words, you can start adding words to its vocabulary. Because I consider warning barks part of a dog's job, I praise a puppy when it begins to react to a car in the driveway or a step on the porch. However, I also chose a breed that doesn't yap all the time, but Dane puppies, like all other puppies, need to learn what to bark at and what to ignore. Thus I soon add the command, THAT'S ENOUGH!, to a pup's vocabulary. I'm not squelching its bark instinct, but I am setting the limits.

Later I add HUSH! IT'S OKAY. Thus, before the pup has figured out what Kent's car sounds like and so barks at Kent's coming home, I teach the OKAY command. Dogs can and should distinguish between friend and foe approaching, but they need help from their people.

Your puppy is listening to you more than you think—and picking up new words!

I cannot emphasize the importance of a command voice enough. The puppy that seems not to be learning basic commands probably isn't hearing those commands as words to take seriously. I've listened as people *nag* their puppies instead of *commanding* them. Just like children, puppies quickly learn to tune out the nagging. The command is short, sharp, and loud. It's direct and simple: *NO. DOWN. SIT. STAY. COME.* Notice that all of these are one-syllable words. The appropriate command isn't, "Fluffy, please sit for me so I can give you a treat." It's "*SIT.*"

Commands are not requests! Before your dog can learn this, you have to know it right to the marrow of your bones. To be in charge, you must use your authority.

And will this use of vocal authority make your dog afraid of you? No, because as soon as the pup has done what you told it to, you'll give hugs, pats, and praises—even treats. Thus for your dog, complying with your commands becomes a fast route to good times.

Similarly, if your pup needs confidence, your tone should be bright, cheerful, and confident. Remember Betty and Bambi at the vet's. Betty's tone was increasing Bambi's unease. Most puppies of the huge breeds go through a shy stage—much like children. It can be embarrassing to have an enormous lout of a Dane at the end of your leash cowering away from some little dustmop of a dog or hiding behind you at the approach of a stranger. Sandy from

Tone of Voice

As much as the words themselves, the tone of your voice conveys meaning to Puppy. Take the simple NO command. I've heard more people than you can imagine unable to rap out a good, credible NO. My friend Eileen Perrault gave me the best advice I've heard on what a NO should sound like.

"Shout it out as if he'd just killed your favorite child!" she said, apropos of some misdeed Cappy had just pulled. Then, knowing me, she added, "Supposing you had a favorite child."

But Eileen's is a good point. If you want to shock your pup into immediate attention, causing it to cease all other activity, your voice quality must override everything else that's on Puppy's mind.

Seattle called me to ask about Frodo's shyness.

"So I have to untangle my watchdog from the bushes where he's hiding," she told me, "and that's not what I expected."

I impressed on Sandy the need to keep getting Frodo out and about, talking cheerfully to him all the time and praising him all over the place for what a swell dog he was. With such treatment, I assured her, he would grow out of his shyness.

Sandy did her job well. Some months after our conversation, she called again to remark that Frodo was all the watchdog she'd ever hoped for—and more. It seems that some man tried to attack Sandy, and Frodo, the former shrinking violet, drove the man away. In fact, Frodo's attack was so convincing, the man was never seen again!

What we're aiming for is that your dog be under your voice command at all times. This won't happen overnight, but as you work on *how* you give commands just as conscientiously as on *what* commands you give, you'll have a dog eventually that responds to every nuance in your tone.

And it has to be *your* voice. Old commands from former owners do not necessarily carry over. We'd had DJ, a marvelously well-educated six-year-old Dane, for about two weeks. A friend, Mike, came for breakfast on Sunday and got into a friendly punning match with Kent. After an especially bad pun from Kent, Mike picked up a newspaper and raised it over his head to swat Kent. From my vantage point, I saw DJ on the couch gathering his muscles, and instantly I knew that the moment that newspaper connected with Kent, DJ would attack Mike.

But DJ wasn't yet under my voice control. Quietly and insistently, I said, "Mike. Freeze. Now."

He heard the urgency in my tone and became a statue. Quickly I crossed to DJ, took hold of his collar, and told him to STAY, a command I knew he'd obey.

A white-faced Mike slowly lowered the newspaper, and we had all learned another page in the story of why working dogs make such incredible family guardians.

The Canine Protector

Basic watchdog training was introduced in Chapter 4 (see page 50). I want to add an additional note here for people who haven't yet made the connection that the canine reaction to danger is to bite. As I've stressed throughout this book, the well-trained puppy grows up to be a dog that loves people and lives amicably with them. Equally unacceptable are the yappy little ankle-biters and the huge attack dogs forever on a hair trigger. But it's unrealistic to pretend that dogs never bite. Your training teaches your puppy not to bite indiscriminately. That's why I'm so strict about not allowing games where the puppy takes the human hand in its mouth and bites, for such games teach the wrong behavior. The puppy who is harshly trained often grows up to be what's called a fear-biter, because human approach has meant danger to this dog since puppyhood. Having had no human friends, the fear-biter bites everyone it can.

Through the centuries of our association with canines, two of the traits people have valued most in their pets have been the tendency to warn of impending danger and that of protecting the human family from danger. We choose what breed puppy we want partly based on how much protection we feel we need. When a dog warns or protects, it is doing its job. I have often told people, "You don't raise a hand in anger to the owner of a Dane and expect to take that hand back unharmed." Both Frodo and DJ were doing what they understood as their job. Frodo connected—as he should have. DJ didn't, because I intervened, and he and Mike very soon became good friends. A large part of our job as owners of dogs is to bring them dependably under our control and not expose them falsely to situations where they consider that we're in danger.

Parents have the responsibility of teaching their children not to rush up to strange dogs. The rushing approach signals danger to puppy or dog, triggering a protective reaction. Although we hope that all dogs are under their owners' control, this is not dependably the case. Children should be taught respect in approaching puppies or dogs—the kind of respect a person ought to show in approaching anyone, human or canine, to whom one hasn't yet been introduced. Many a well-meaning dog has been sentenced to death because ill-mannered children provoked its natural protective reaction and then their parents cried "Foul!"

As your puppy matures, not only will it understand every nuance of your voice and body language, it will also take many of its cues from your unspoken feelings. Blitz was a nervous rider until I conquered my nervousness in unfamiliar, traffic-choked cities, because he was taking his cues from my nonverbal behavior.

Recently I got a review of how closely tuned dogs can be to the inner feelings of their owners. A bratty eleven-year-old boy was visiting us with his parents. He quickly destroyed a dog toy he found lying around, broke another toy Kent gave him to play with, and was obviously looking for more damage to do. I felt my anger rising, but I got distracted for a moment or so. The next thing I saw, the boy was standing very quietly in a corner of the room. Cordy (my young blue Dane) was standing perhaps three feet from the boy, eyeing him intently. Instantly I got the message. Cordy was doing what social conventions barred me from doing—he was disciplining an unruly child! However, how drastic Cordy's methods might be I neither knew nor wanted to discover.

"You'll be just fine," I told the boy steadily, "as long as you just stand quietly for a minute." By the size of the boy's eyes, I knew he was listening.

I put Cordy's collar on him, snapped a leash to it, patted Cordy, and asked Kent whether he'd put the blue boy in his pen. From the look on my face, Kent understood what was up, and Cordy went to his pen. Later Kent told me that he'd praised Cordy all the way.

As I've said, Cordy is an unusually dominant Dane. Though he's learned that Kent and I outrank him in our home pack, he considers himself right up there with us when it comes to maintaining law and order. My experience has been that it's the dominant dogs that are most closely tuned to their owners' emotions— and the ones most likely to take action when they think the owner needs help.

Any dog trainer will tell you that dogs react negatively to sneaking or stealthy behavior. They instinctively feel impending danger and tense up in preparation. They work from non-verbal cues. If you're nervous, frightened, or hostile, your well-bonded dog knows this and prepares to protect you. You may say "It's ALL RIGHT," but if you don't feel that the situation is all right, your dog isn't fooled for a minute. Any time you find your well-trained puppy (or dog) reacting as to danger, and you don't recognize the cause, check yourself. What cues are you giving? We humans do some strange things that

dogs would never understand, like inviting to our homes people we loathe but need to curry favor with for some financial or social reason. We paste false smiles on our faces and do the socially correct thing— but our beloved canine protector hears the voice within us that is seething with resentment at having to behave so falsely. And the canine protector may very well decide to remedy our distress by eliminating its cause!

You can always discover the person you dislike in a group; your dog will tell you! Generally, in a social situation, your pet will simply avoid the unwelcome guest. But many men who make unwelcome advances to women have had their advances strongly rebuffed by the resident canine protector!

In summary, it's vital to train our protectors to recognize when we need protection and when we don't. Prudence on our part dictates that our dogs never bite except under extreme provocation, and even then, in our litigation-happy society, we may regret that we were protected. Ellen's dog attacked the intruder who was threatening her two-year-old child, and the intruder had the gall to sue! He lost, but he's not unique.

On the other hand, people who have ill intentions toward anyone protected by a well-socialized canine guardian should—and do— know that they're taking their chances. That's why families with good dogs make poor targets for thieves and intruders.

Fun and Games

Along with learning its responsibilities and duties, Puppy is also open to learning whatever tricks and games you want to teach. But before you decide to teach Puppy any game—or to let some cute puppy behavior continue—ask yourself whether what you think is cute now will be cute in a full-grown dog.

Though we refuse to allow Dane puppies to jump on us or anyone else, Kent and I think it's fun to have an adult Dane who puts its paws on our shoulders and comes up for a visit. So once a puppy is full grown, won't be putting too much strain on its rear end, and has the sense to obey commands, we begin the UP lessons, squatting down at first and putting the dog's forepaws on our shoulders as we say, Sombre, UP! Eventually, all we have to do is pat our shoulders and say UP, and the Dane comes up in one clean

The basic theory of this game is . . .

movement. This is never done except on command.

With Caesar, who hadn't been taught not to jump on people at will, I changed his jumping to behavior big dogs aren't noted for—I taught him to sit on his haunches and put his forepaws on my belly. Before long, Caesar sat up with no support whenever he wanted to be cute.

Dogs of all breeds will FETCH, BRING, and GIVE. Especially if you've got a sporting dog that you might hunt with someday, teach the GIVE or DROP IT command at the same time you teach FETCH. Otherwise, you'll spend your hunting days chasing down your dog to get the birds you thought you were going to have for supper!

The point is, once you've taught the basics, you can teach your pup anything that works well to amuse you both, bond you, and make your lives together happier. The more you are your pup's teacher, the more firmly your pup looks to you as the alpha of the pack. As your puppy knows more, it welcomes advanced lessons, be they lessons about what games you like to play or what jobs you want it to do. Just like children, albeit on a more limited scale, the puppy thrives on going beyond the basics. While you stick firmly to consistency, in things like feeding times and obeying certain commands, you and your maturing puppy can cope with varying amounts of inconsistency. It is in these areas of innovation that you allow your pup's own unique personality to blossom.

Rewarding Work

Many people find great fulfillment in obedience training their dogs. I've mentioned a basic obedience course as a necessity for anyone who's going to raise a civilized puppy, but one can go far beyond the basics. It all depends on what you want. Watching a well-trained obedience dog work is a pleasure, and in dog shows, it's the obedience ring where you'll see the real honesty of dog and owner functioning as a team. You can go beyond obedience into tracking, too. One doesn't have to have a bloodhound to participate in this sport; I've seen Danes put in excellent tracking performances. The puppy who has been taught the game of GO FIND can grow up to GO FIND in a very serious way. Dogsledding is becoming an increasingly popular sport. If you've ever watched well-trained herding dogs work, you know what precision they exhibit, and you can guess at the time and love it took to train them.

The more you learn about your puppy and its breed, the more you'll see that your horizons are limited only by how much time and expense you want to invest in having fun with your canine companion.

Not Attack

The one kind of canine behavior I have always seriously discouraged is attack training. There are pathetically few people equipped to deal with the dangers of living with a

A well-trained sheepdog at work.

fully-trained attack dog. Some basically very nice breeds of dogs have been ruined by owners who decided to turn them into something they weren't intended to be—hair-trigger attackers. I think of what's been done to rottweilers, for instance, a breed as gentle and cooperative as Danes, yet today suffering from a reputation as aggressive, fierce dogs. Or American Staffordshires, more commonly called pit bulls and actually banned in some communities, all because too many people decided to turn their loyal pets into macho dogs.

There have always been people who, for various neurotic reasons, have needed to display their own violent and aggressive tendencies through their dogs. Serious, caring dog breeders need to be strict in their refusal to sell to such people whenever they can identify them, just as humane societies and other animal adoption agencies need to turn such people away from dog ownership. A small group of people—such

This Labrador retriever has been trained to search for avalanche victims.

as the Schutzhund clubs—are equipped to train and own attack dogs for various civic and law-enforcement reasons. In my experience, such groups carefully police their own. But, as you can see from example after example that I've given throughout this book, if what you want is a puppy who will grow up and protect its family, there are two easy basic steps to achieve this goal:

1. Choose the correct breed of dog.
2. Take that puppy into your home, love and educate it.

You'll have all the protection you could ever hope for!

Never Acceptable

Some behavior is never acceptable from any dog, regardless of the breed or the circumstances. Most of the unacceptable behavior is marginally amusing in a puppy, and unfortunately many people laugh at such puppy behavior and then end up having to take the adult dog

to a pound or have it otherwise destroyed. I see three major behaviors as always unacceptable.

1. Growling at the owner. Sure, it's funny to have a little fuzzball growl at you like a miniature buzz-saw. Knock that behavior off right away. A quick sharp smack *under* the muzzle, coupled with a loud NO! will get rid of the growling. Growling is serious, hostile behavior. It's a threat. The adult dog will growl at an intruder or an attacker without having to be taught, as this is instinctive. But *never* should this threat be used against an owner.

2. Biting or nipping at the human hand or arm. Again, many people play with a small puppy's mouth, encouraging it to nip with its sharp little baby teeth. How is the adult dog going to know that it's wrong to bite hands and arms unless it's been taught? Just as for growling, the smack under the muzzle and the NO are immediate corrections. When it is time to take a human hand into its mouth, a dog must do it seriously—and every family protector will do so should the situation warrant.

3. Refusing to let the owner reach into the pup's mouth. As owner, you're alpha. You make the decisions, like when you might need to pry Puppy's mouth open to remove some object it shouldn't have or that could kill it. During Puppy's life, you, as well as your

vet, are going to have to give it pills, too, and you need access to Puppy's mouth whenever you choose. Start early. Take a toy away from Puppy before it's done with it, just to establish that you have the right to do so. Take a bone away when you decide Puppy's chewed it long enough. Always praise and pat Puppy afterward, establishing that this is behavior that you like.

When Cappy was still a growing Dane, the kind of calcium we used for him came in raspberry-flavored pills. He got 12 of those at a time! Our friend Tony took Cappy out on a long show trip and used to delight in inviting other handlers over to his rig in the evening to watch him give pills to the big puppy. Plagued with crabby little dogs who fought even one tiny tablet, other handlers were distinctly envious of Tony who had only to approach Cappy, say "Pill time!," and have him open his mouth and gulp down the whole handful of calcium pills.

On the other hand, no one was envious when Cappy spat an entire mouthful of rice all over the place during the time some dunce had advised us to force-feed him rice to put show weight on him!

Listen to Your Dog

Even as you have a great deal to tell your puppy in the way of training advice before s/he grows to adult-

How your dog holds its ears often tells you a lot about what it's thinking.

hood, so also your pup will increasingly have much to tell you. There are the simple, obvious messages, like "I have to go out." There's the more subtle "I don't feel good." And there may be "I don't like this person I've just met." As long as your puppy is giving you that message in a civilized way—that is, not immediately leaping on the stranger and attacking for no reason—listen to the message. Don't force all strangers on your puppy. Dogs deserve the respect of being able to keep their distance from people they distrust. My experience has been that the distrust has always had good reason. Friends of mine were burgled by an acquaintance whom their dog had always avoided. How did they know who the burglar was? When they came home from the movies, the man was on the floor, the dog standing guard over him. He actually begged for the police.

When your well-trained puppy does something utterly out of character, pay attention. Something is wrong. You are being given an important message. Heidi was a wonderful field companion, and my friend John, the botanist, asked whether he could take her along on a long, lonely collecting trip into the desert. When they returned, John was enthusiastic in his praise of Heidi.

"She saved my life," he told me. "At first I was annoyed with her when she blocked my path and refused to let me go forward. But as soon as I discovered that she was warning me away from rattlers, I paid attention to her."

Nobody taught Heidi that behavior. But because she loved John and was responsible for him in the field, she took her duties seriously.

Yes, I realize that I have occasionally indicated that dogs will and do attack people. The well-socialized, properly trained dog never does that except when it's absolutely necessary. That's why many criminals avoid the person guarded by a serious dog that knows its job.

Ask for Help

The whole genesis of this book comes from the days when I was breeding and selling puppies. I always sent home pages of written instructions, but I also emphasized that I was always available for phone calls about unexpected or unexplained behavior in the puppies.

"No question is too trivial," I said. "What looks minor to you now might be a sign of some problem that could become major." And I still get the phone calls. You'll note that I haven't been shy in the Foreword about where I live, and a number of my readers have phoned with questions. I'd rather spend time answering questions or trying to assess problems than have a good dog go to the pound because its owner couldn't figure out some unexpected behavior!

The good dog trainers that I know feel the same way. Do not fret and stew over something your puppy or dog is doing. Get help. Books like this are fine. Dependable breeders who know dogs like yours are excellent. Obedience trainers are great. There are some dog trainers who make house calls. I think of Delilah, who gives personalized instruction to dogs and their owners. She figured out why one dog was madly attacking the door everytime anyone came to visit, and she taught the owner how to modify such unacceptable behavior.

Of course, take your puppy through at least one obedience class.

A new source of help shows up on the Internet, as well as on many other electronic online services. I often drop in on a conference known as Dogs. Behavior, as do a number of other dog behaviorists. Though you won't get the hands-on assistance you'd get from the actual presence of a person, you will get fast response, and often a lot of it. Quality varies. Use your good sense in trying new methods!

Level of Perfection

In the final analysis, it's your puppy and your decision: Just how well civilized does your dog need to be? I used to include at the bottom of my rules sheet for obedience classes this sentence: EVERYONE HAS THE DOG THEY WANT AND DESERVE. Many people got immediately motivated to be serious about training after they thought a moment about that statement.

I insist on my dogs obeying commands for three basic reasons:

1. well enough to save their lives.
2. well enough not to hurt people.
3. well enough to stay out of danger.

When I've achieved that level of perfection, I'm quite happy to live with a little looniness.

If the strategies I've shared in this book let you bring a puppy along to whatever level of perfection *you like to live with,* then my aim is achieved, for I truly hate to see dogs doomed to the pound because no one thought to teach their owners to civilize them when they were puppies. This civilizing process is absolutely a win-win situation, for both you and your puppy will be rewarded with a lifetime of love and good times together.

Puppy love—does anyone ever really deserve it?

Bibliography

Anderson, Robert, DVM, and Barbara J. Wrede: *Caring for Older Cats & Dogs* (Williamson, Charlotte, Vermont, 1990). Though the title might strike you as not applicable to you and your puppy, this book gives you good information about nutrition, as well as alerting you to toxins in your pet's environment. The last chapter talks about starting right to prepare a young pet for a long, healthy life.

Baer, Ted: *Communicating with Your Dog* (Barron's, Hauppauge, New York, 1989). An excellent resource to show you how to extend your dog's active vocabulary. You'll open amazing horizons of learning for both your pet and yourself as you put Baer's lessons to use.

Lorenz, Konrad: *King Solomon's Ring* (Crowell, 1952). The key to your being able to thoroughly civilize your puppy is being able to think like a dog. Lorenz gives us insights into canine mentality.

——— . *Man Meets Dog* (Penguin, 1965). This is the PhD of learning to think like a dog! You'll find out whether you've really been the leader of any dog you've ever owned, and you'll learn how to become the admired leader of your present pup.

Mowat, Farley: *Never Cry Wolf* (Bantam, 1983). Many of the destructive myths about dogs are dispelled as a sideline of this examination of the true nature of wolves. It's another resource for you in discovering how the canine mind works.

Pearsall, Milo and Charles G. Leedham: *Dog Obedience Training* (Charles Scribner's Sons, n.d.). Compassionate, thorough, and effective, the training methods described will enable you to teach your dog without breaking its spirit.

Study the experts to keep up with your puppy's expanding horizons.

Wrede, Barbara J.: *Before You Buy That Puppy* (Barron's, Hauppauge, New York, 1994). Everything the new or prospective dog owner needs to know about selecting and preparing for the new arrival, and then helping it adapt to its new family.

But don't neglect me while you have your nose in a book!

There are countless wonderful dog stories, canine health books, books on individual breeds of dogs and their special characteristics, and books on specialized kinds of training. You'll develop your own list of favorites, to be read and savored after a busy day enjoying life with your canine companion. But no book can replace the rewards of living with a well-civilized dog!

Photo Credits

Barbara Augello: pages x, 5, 18 bottom, 20, 43, 47, 61, 72, 75, 76, 95, 96, 103, 105, 106, 107.

Ted Baer: pages 7 bottom, 9, 11, 30 bottom, 32, 33, 36, 48, 49, 54, 55, 60, 68, 80, 85, 88.

Michele Early Bridges: pages 10, 19.

Gary Ellis: pages 1, 18 top, 30 top, 44, 63, 84, 100.

D.J. Hamer: page 52.

Judith E. Strom: front cover, inside front cover, pages 3, 4, 6, 7 top, 8, 12, 14, 15, 16, 17, 22, 29, 39, 41, 45, 50, 51, 53, 57, 59, 64, 65, 66, 70, 73, 74, 76, 78, 79, 86, 94, 101, 102, inside back cover, back cover.

Index